Kayak Fishing for Beginners:

The Ultimate Starter Guide to Gear, Techniques, Safety, and Ethical Angling

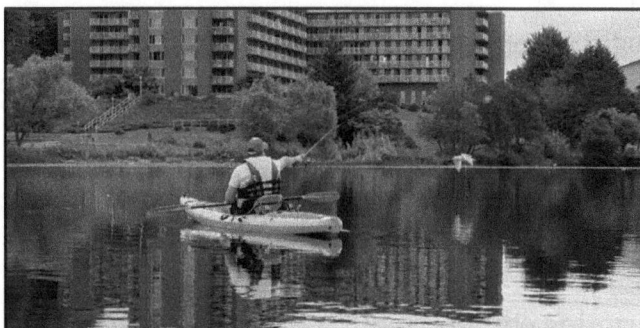

by

Morgan Williams

Bzik Publishing LLC

Seattle, WA

Morgan Williams

Printed and published in the United States of America by Bzik Publishing LLC.

First printing edition 2024.

All inquiries about this book can be sent to the author via publisher.

Email: BzikPublishing@gmail.com

Bzik Publishing LLC

Seattle, WA

Table of Contents

Introduction

Hello fellow anglers.

In this book, I hope to provide you with a starting point for your kayak fishing adventure. Be warned, kayak fishing is fun and addictive, and you will get hooked (no pun intended?) on how exciting fishing from a kayak can be. The thrill of hooking into a large fish and having it pull you is a feeling like no other. The ability to stealthily sneak up on wildlife and the calmness of hearing the waves lapping against your kayak's hull while nature surrounds you are all memories that will become engrained in your mind.

This sport is not just about catching fish; it's about embracing the great outdoors, enjoying peaceful moments on the water, and experiencing the thrill of the catch from a whole new perspective. So, grab your kayak, paddle, and fishing gear, and prepare for a journey that promises not just trophies but memories, too. Let's embark on the world of kayak fishing together. Fun, surprises, and the joy of the catch await!

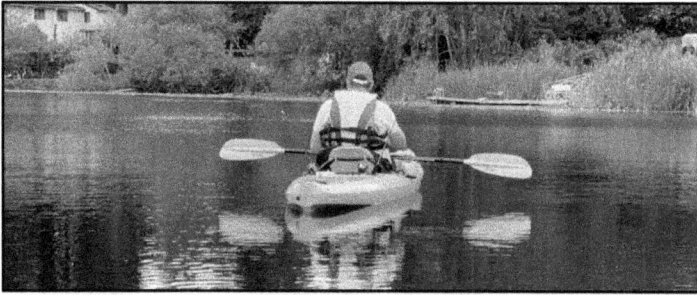

Author kayaking on an urban lake

I first got into kayak fishing when my fishing boat did not start, and I was several miles from the boat launch. Luckily, another boater was amazing enough to tow me to the launch. Turns out my engine would not start due to a $5 part – a fuse. I would not have been able to change it even if I had the part due to the location of the fuse and the tools needed to complete the repair. This, and several other minor issues, caused me to look for a better, more reliable, and cheaper way to fish. A memory from years prior popped back into my mind. I was on a family vacation to Lake George in New York. I went fishing with my uncle, and on that trip, I hooked into a large pike, which pulled my kayak and I from eighteen inches of water to 30+ feet of water. Talk about a rush for a pre-teen being pulled by a fish in a boat. This memory stuck in my mind over the years and was reintroduced and set into reality following my negative boat experience that one day.

Years later, enter my first kayak. I got it secondhand from someone who didn't have the time to use it. Lucky me! I had been looking into how much it would cost to start kayak fishing at a sporting goods store the day before. I got this new-to-me kayak, a 14-foot Wilderness Systems Tarpon, for half the price of what I found in the store. The kayak I purchased even came with an upgraded seat, paddle, and life vest. I got quite the deal. This began my ongoing task of changing from a motorboat fisher to a kayak fisher. During this transition, I quickly realized that I did not have the opportunity to bring with me the vast array of tackle and rods and reels that I did on my boat. Granted, I could, but would sacrifice weight and the ability to safely, with my beginning skill level, access the added gear. Would I like it? Would it live up to the hype that I made it in my head? Would it live up to the memories that I had growing up?

BEST. DECISION. EVER.

The following chapters will include sections on gear, safety, and techniques. This approach will help you easily navigate through the information, applying it as you go along on your adventures. You may ask yourself, "Why do I need to change from a motorboat to a non-motorized kayak?" Here are a few of my favorite reasons.

- Kayaks are significantly less expensive than motorized boats. There are no fuel costs, lower (to no) maintenance costs, and often no need for expensive mooring fees or trailers, making kayak fishing an affordable option for many.

- Kayaks can access shallow waters, narrow channels, and tight spots where larger boats cannot go. This allows anglers to fish in secluded or densely vegetated areas, increasing their chances of catching fish in untouched waters. You can launch your kayak virtually anywhere that is safe and accessible. There is no need for a boat launch.

- Kayaks are much quieter than motorized boats, making it easier to approach skittish fish without startling them. Their stealthy nature can be a significant advantage when targeting species easily spooked by noise.

- Kayaks do not use fuel and produce no emissions, making them a more environmentally friendly option. Compared to motorized boats, they also cause minimal disturbance to aquatic ecosystems.

- Kayak fishing provides a good physical workout, as paddling is involved in moving from one spot to another. It can be a rewarding way to combine fitness with leisure.

- Kayaks are easier to transport and store than motorized boats. They can often be carried on a vehicle roof rack, requiring less storage space when not in use.

- The independence from fuel reduces costs and eliminates the worry about fuel availability or mechanical failures associated with engines, making kayak fishing more reliable in remote areas.

This is by no means a book that will provide all that kayak fishing is. There are some kayakers who have their kayaks rigged with enough equipment to make motor-boaters jealous. Think gas engines, outriggers, downriggers, full electronic displays, batteries, etc. While there is absolutely nothing wrong with this type of rigging and kayak fishing, I prefer to keep it simple, efficient, and inexpensive. This keep-it-simple approach has worked well for me for over 20 years in freshwater, saltwater, and brackish, and I see no reason to change. Enjoy.

1. Getting Started with Kayak Fishing

Choosing Your First Kayak: SOT vs. SIK Pros and Cons

Kayak fishing offers an intimate connection with the aquatic environment, unmatched by larger watercraft. The choice of your first kayak, therefore, is not merely about purchasing a piece of equipment; it's about selecting a companion for these serene and invigorating experiences. This chapter aims to guide you through the essential first step of your kayak fishing adventure— choosing the right kayak. With a focus on the two primary types of kayaks, Sit-On-Top (SOT) and Sit-In Kayak (SIK), this section will explore the advantages of each, helping you make an informed decision based on your personal needs, environmental conditions, and financial considerations.

What type of kayak is best for you? You will have to answer that question yourself. Typically, there are two types of kayaks: **Sit-On-Top** (SOT) and **Sit-In Kayak** (SIK). Both have pros and cons, which can determine which you prefer. I prefer a SOT kayak. This is what I learned to kayak with, and it is what I am most comfortable using.

Sit-on-top kayaks offer several benefits that make them particularly popular for fishing. Here are a few reasons why people prefer them to Sit-In Kayaks.

+ <u>Ease of Entry and Exit</u>: SOT kayaks have an open deck, which makes it easy to get on and off the kayak. This is particularly useful when you're launching from the shore.

+ <u>Self-Draining</u>: SOT kayaks have scupper holes that allow water that splashes onto the deck to drain out automatically. This feature keeps the kayak from filling with water, enhancing safety and comfort.

+ <u>Stability</u>: SOT kayaks are generally wider than traditional sit-inside kayaks, providing a stable platform. This stability is crucial when fishing as it allows for standing up to cast and reel in fish, which can be difficult in less stable kayaks.

+ <u>Storage Space</u>: SOT kayaks often come with ample storage space, including open wells and hatches that can hold fishing gear, coolers, and personal belongings. The accessible layout lets anglers easily reach their equipment.

+ Durability: Typically made from hardy materials like polyethylene, SOT kayaks are durable and can handle being dragged across beaches and bumping into rocks without significant damage.

+ Versatility: They can be used in various water conditions, including lakes, rivers, and coastal waters. The versatility extends to activities beyond fishing, such as diving and snorkeling, where easy water access is important.

+ Customization: SOT kayaks often feature accessory rails and mounting points for fishing rods, GPS units, and other gear, allowing anglers to customize their setup based on their needs.

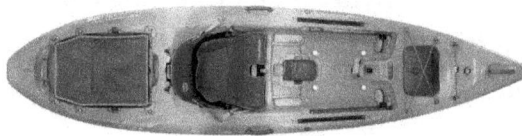

Wilderness System Tarpon

Ascend FS128T

Overall, the combination of stability, ease of use, and adaptability makes sit-on-top kayaks particularly well-suited for fishing and other water activities. With all those positives, there are also negatives.

- Exposure to the Elements: In a SOT kayak, you are more exposed to the sun, wind, and water. This can lead to sunburn, faster dehydration, or getting colder quicker in windy conditions. The lack of an enclosed cockpit also means you're more likely to get wet from splashing water.

- Heavier Weight: SOT kayaks are generally heavier than sit-inside models, which can make them more challenging to transport and handle on land. The extra weight is due to their wider and often more feature-rich design.

- Less Efficient Paddling: Due to their wider hull design for increased stability, SOT kayaks can be less efficient to paddle. They typically create more drag and are slower than narrower, sit-inside kayaks, making them less ideal for covering long distances.

- Limited Performance in Rough Water: While SOT kayaks are stable, their open design can be a disadvantage in choppy water or strong currents. Water entering the kayak will drain out through scupper holes, but it can be unsettling and uncomfortable.

- Higher Wind Resistance: The higher profile of SOT kayaks can catch more wind, which can make paddling in windy conditions more challenging and exhausting.

- Cost: SOT kayaks designed for fishing often come with many built-in features like rod holders, gear tracks, and storage options. While these features are convenient, they can also make the kayaks more expensive than more basic models. It is possible to find "bare bones" kayaks and add these items later.

These drawbacks don't necessarily overshadow the benefits for every user, but they are important to consider based on your specific needs, paddling locations, and conditions.

Sit-inside (SIK) kayaks offer several distinct advantages, especially in certain environments and conditions, which can make them preferable for kayak fishing under specific circumstances. Here are several reasons why people prefer Sit-In Kayaks over Sit-On-Top kayaks...

+ <u>Protection from the Elements</u>: One of the primary advantages of SIK kayaks is the protection they offer from the wind, water, and sun. Being partially enclosed helps keep you dry and warmer, particularly in cooler or windy weather, which can be crucial in extending fishing sessions comfortably.

+ <u>Efficiency in Paddling</u>: SIK kayaks are typically more streamlined than SOT kayaks, which makes them easier to paddle over longer distances. This efficiency is beneficial for fishing in larger lakes or rivers, where you need to cover a larger area to find fish.

+ <u>Lower Center of Gravity</u>: The seating position in a SIK kayak is lower, which reduces the center of gravity and can increase overall stability in the water. This can be especially important in rougher water, where wave action is a factor.

+ <u>Reduced Wind Resistance</u>: Due to their lower profile, sit-inside kayaks are less affected by wind compared to the higher profiles of SOT kayaks. This makes them easier to manage in windy conditions and can reduce paddling fatigue.

+ <u>Lighter Weight</u>: SIK kayaks are generally lighter than SOT kayaks, making them easier to transport and carry to the water. This can be a significant advantage if you frequently need to carry your kayak over long distances by hand.

+ <u>Potential for Customization</u>: While not as inherently equipped as many SOT kayaks, many sit-inside models can be customized with fishing accessories like rod holders, GPS units, and fish finders. Enthusiasts often modify their cockpits and decks to suit their specific fishing needs.

+ <u>Storage</u>: Sit-inside kayaks often have built-in covered storage compartments fore and aft, which can protect gear from the elements better than the open storage areas typically found on SOT kayaks.

Pelican Argo 100x

SIK kayaks are often preferred for their performance in colder climates or more challenging water conditions, where the paddler's comfort and handling are priorities. They are particularly well-suited for anglers who prioritize long paddling efficiency and protection from cold and wet conditions over the ease of entry and extreme stability offered by SOT designs.

Again, a sit-in kayak has negatives, as do sit-on-top kayaks. Sit-inside (SIK) kayaks, while offering several benefits for fishing, also have certain drawbacks that could affect their suitability depending on the fishing conditions and the angler's preferences.

- Limited Mobility: Due to the enclosed cockpit, movement in a SIK kayak is more restricted. This can make moving around, stretching, or shifting positions harder, which might be necessary during long fishing trips. This is especially true if you are taller and like/need to bend your legs for comfort.

- Difficulty in Re-Entry: Re-entering can be much more challenging than a sit-on-top (SOT) kayak if a SIK kayak capsizes. Water fills the cockpit, and you generally need to get to shore or have a bilge pump handy to empty the water before you can get back in safely.

- Exposure in Rough Water: Although the enclosed design helps protect against the elements, in rough water, water entering the cockpit can stay there unless it's manually removed, adding to the risk and discomfort. Cockpit covers are available for many SIK.

- Limited Space for Gear: Sit-inside kayaks often have secure storage compartments. The space is usually more confined and less accessible than on a sit-on-top kayak. This can be a drawback when you need quick access to various pieces of fishing gear.

- <u>Lower Visibility</u>: The lower seating position in a SIK can reduce visibility compared to the higher seating position of a SOT kayak. This can be a disadvantage when spotting fish or navigating in densely vegetated areas or overgrown waters.

- <u>Comfort and Accessibility</u>: The enclosed cockpit can also be less comfortable for larger individuals or those who prefer more open space, and it can also be less accessible for individuals with mobility issues.

- <u>Less Stability for Active Fishing</u>: While sit-inside kayaks can be quite stable, the lower profile and enclosed space can make them feel less stable when performing actions like casting and reeling, especially for beginners or those not accustomed to the dynamics of a SIK.

These factors make sit-inside kayaks less ideal for casual, warm-weather fishing or for anglers who prioritize ease of use and accessibility over paddling efficiency and protection from the elements. With all those factors being listed, it is up to you to decide which kayak style is best for you. Both styles can be customized in various ways to allow for successful fishing. It is merely a preference as to which one you want to go with to enjoy your time fishing in. Understanding your specific needs and the unique characteristics of each kayak type will help ensure that your choice enhances your fishing experiences, making each trip productive and enjoyable. A final aspect to consider is the size of the person the kayak will be for. A larger person will cause greater water displacement. In a SOT kayak, water could enter through the scupper holes. This should not be a deciding factor, though, as there are scupper plugs you can purchase to prevent water from entering through these holes.

Variety of Scupper Plugs

2. Selecting a Paddle

Tips and Information to Select the Proper Paddle

While not the kayak itself, the paddle is an essential factor that warrants additional detail. When selecting a paddle for kayak fishing, several key features should be considered to enhance your experience and effectiveness on the water. Below are the main features to look for.

- Length: The correct length of a paddle is crucial for efficient paddling. It depends on your height and the width of your kayak. Typically, taller individuals or those with wider kayaks will need longer paddles. Most fishing kayaks are wider, so paddles often range from 240 cm to 260 cm (94 inches to 102 inches) in length. A paddle that's too long or too short can lead to inefficient strokes and increased fatigue.

KAYAK WIDTH	UNDER 23"	23" - 28"	28" - 32"	32" OR MORE
PADDLER HEIGHT	Recommended Paddle Length			
UNDER 5'	200 cm	210 cm	220 cm	230 cm
5' TO 5'6"	210 cm	220 cm	230 cm	240 cm
5'7" TO 6'	220 cm	220 cm	230 cm	240 cm
6' OR TALLER	220 cm	230 cm	240 cm	250 cm

The guidelines above are based only on the width of a kayak. There may be other factors to consider when choosing paddle length.

- Blade Shape: Blades come in various shapes, each designed for specific paddling conditions. For fishing, you'll likely want a blade that balances power and stroke efficiency. The paddle blade's shape and size affect your strokes' power and cadence. Wider blades provide more power per stroke, which is beneficial in strong currents or when quick acceleration is needed. Narrower blades allow for a higher paddling cadence, which can be more efficient over long distances.
- Material: Paddles can be made from various materials, impacting weight, durability, and cost. Common materials include:
  Aluminum: Durable and affordable but heavier, which can lead to faster fatigue.
  Fiberglass: A good balance of weight, durability, and cost. Lighter than aluminum but typically more expensive.
  Carbon Fiber: Lightweight and efficient but the most expensive. Ideal for those who spend long hours on the water, as it reduces paddling fatigue.
- Weight: A lighter paddle reduces fatigue over long periods, which is crucial for kayak fishing, where you may be on the water for several hours at a

time. However, lighter materials like carbon fiber are more expensive.

- Shaft Type: Shafts can be straight or bent. Bent shafts can reduce strain on your wrists and improve the efficiency of each paddle stroke. Some shafts are also adjustable, allowing you to change the length based on conditions and personal preference.

Bent Shaft vs. Straight Shaft

- Feathering: Many paddles offer adjustable feathering, where the blades can be set at different angles relative to each other. This feature allows you to customize the paddle for wind conditions and personal paddling style, potentially reducing wind resistance and wrist fatigue.
- Breakdown Capability: A paddle that breaks down into two or more pieces is easier to transport and store. For kayak fishermen, having a spare paddle is also advisable, and breakdown paddles can be stored as compact spares.

- Grip: Comfortable grips are essential, especially when paddling for a long time. Look for paddles with ergonomic grips or those that can be customized with grip tape to enhance comfort and control.

- Color: Bright colors can improve visibility on the water for safety, especially in areas with heavy boat traffic.

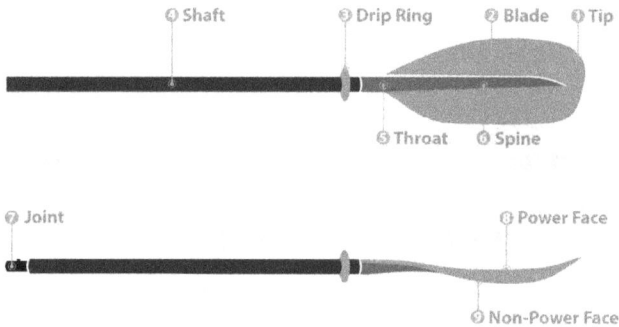

Parts of a Kayak Paddle

When choosing a paddle for kayak fishing, consider how and where you fish and your physical needs. This will ensure you select a paddle that enhances your fishing experience and comfort on the water. A great article was written on angleoar.com by Meg McCall: *What is the best kayak paddle to buy?* This article provides a great deal of information to help you determine what paddle is best for you. It is worth taking the time to read it.

When kayak fishing, many anglers focus on selecting the right kayak and fishing gear, often overlooking the significance of a good paddle. However, the paddle is your primary means of propulsion and control on the water, making it an essential component of your fishing experience. Investing in a good kayak paddle is not just about owning quality equipment; it's about enhancing every aspect of your kayak fishing experience. A suitable paddle increases your efficiency on the water, reduces physical strain, and allows for better control of your kayak. As you select your paddle, consider your specific needs, the typical conditions you will encounter, and how each feature will impact your time on the water. Remember, the right paddle is as essential to your kayak fishing success as the right lure or fishing rod.

3. Essential Gear for the Kayak Angler

Items to Maintain Safety on Your Kayaking Trip

A kayak fishing adventure is an exhilarating way to connect with nature and enjoy the thrill of the catch. However, safety should always be your top priority when heading out on the water. Equipping yourself with the right safety gear not only ensures your well-being but also enhances your overall experience. Below is a suggested list of essential safety items every kayak angler should have.

Onyx Personal Flotation Device

- Personal Flotation Device (PFD): The Personal Flotation Device (PFD) stands paramount as a safety requirement and as a fundamental piece of gear that ensures security and peace of mind.

Selecting a PFD designed explicitly for fishing is important. It offers buoyancy and accommodates the full range of motion necessary for fishing-related actions. Unlike standard life jackets, fishing PFDs often come with additional features such as pockets for tackle and loops for hanging small tools, enhancing your efficiency and accessibility to gear while on the water. The importance of comfort cannot be overstated; a well-fitting PFD should feel like a part of your angling attire, not a cumbersome addition. It should fit snugly without restricting breathing or movement, allowing for prolonged periods of wear without discomfort. Remember, the correct PFD is your first line of defense against the inherent risks of water sports, and, as such, choosing one should be a deliberate decision informed by quality, fit, and suitability for the kayak fishing environment.

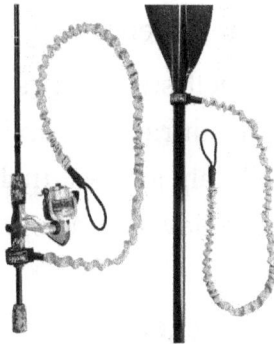

Gear Leash

- Gear Leash: Leashes, for both your paddle and gear, are tethers that attach your gear to your kayak. A paddle leash secures your paddle to your kayak, preventing it from floating away if you drop it. This is crucial for maintaining your ability to navigate and control the kayak, especially in strong currents or windy conditions. You can also attach leashes to your gear to prevent losing them if you do capsize.

- Signal Whistle/ Visual Signaling Device: A whistle is a simple, effective tool for signaling for help. It can be heard over long distances and works even when you're exhausted or hypothermic. Items like flares, signal mirrors, or a high-visibility flag can attract attention during emergencies, aiding rescue efforts. Depending on your local boating requirements, these items may also be required to have on board. Check with your local Department of Wildlife and Fisheries for a complete list of kayak safety requirements.

- First Aid Kit: A well-stocked first aid kit allows you to handle minor injuries or stabilize more serious conditions until help arrives. Include bandages, antiseptic, pain relievers, and specific medication if needed.

- Bilge Pump or Sponge: Water can accumulate in your kayak due to waves, rain, or splashes. These tools remove water that may enter the kayak.

Keeping the cockpit dry helps prevent capsizing and maintains stability. One or both are necessary if you fish in a SIK.

Clip On Navigation Lights

- Headlamp, Waterproof Flashlight, and/or Navigation Light: If you plan to be on the water during low-light conditions (dawn, dusk, or night), navigation lights make you visible to other vessels, reducing the risk of collisions. Flashlights and/or headlamps can signal for help, navigate in the dark, and manage your fishing gear. Navigation lights are raised above the water, allowing for visibility to other boaters as seen from a distance. The red/green shows an oncoming boater the direction of your kayak. The white masthead light shows other boaters your location and can be seen from a great distance at night. This may be a requirement for safety, depending on your local laws.

- Knife or Multi-tool: A sharp knife or multi-tool can be used in various situations, such as cutting tangled fishing lines, repairing gear, or emergencies. These are just good to have in general. Sometimes a screw needs to be tightened on your reel, or you get a lure tangled in a random rope.

- Sun Protection (Sunscreen, Hat, Sunglasses, Clothing, etc.): Direct sun exposure can lead to sunburns, heatstroke, and long-term skin damage. Protective clothing and sunscreen help mitigate these risks.

- Appropriate Clothing: Depending on the conditions, wearing layers of quick-drying clothing and possibly a wetsuit or drysuit helps regulate your body temperature and protects against hypothermia or overheating.

- Float Plan: Before heading out, inform someone about your destination, expected return time, and who to contact if you do not return as scheduled. This ensures that someone knows your whereabouts and can initiate a search if necessary. This is another non-negotiable for me when I go fishing. It is always good for people to know where and when you plan to return.

- Navigation Tools (GPS or Compass and Map): These help you find your way, especially in unfamiliar or extensive water bodies. A GPS can provide precise location details, while a traditional compass and map are reliable without batteries. Many modern phones already have this type of technology built in. Familiarize yourself with your technology before purchasing equipment that you may already have. Ensure you know how to use this type of tech before venturing into unknown areas.

Scotty Rod Holder and Flush Mount Rod Holder

- Rod Holders: While not necessarily safety gear, rod holders keep your deck and seating free of clutter, preventing potential safety issues. Depending on the kayak, these may have already been installed. If not, don't worry; there are many options for installing them yourself. Two typical types for kayak fishing are adjustable Rod Holders and Flush-Mount Rod holders. Both have pros and cons, as each caters to different fishing styles and setups. I have both on my kayak. I have Flush Mount Rod holders behind my seat in order to store my poles while paddling to keep them out of the way. In addition, I have an Adjustable Rod Holder mounted in front of me. I use this one when trolling to see my pole while paddling or moving short distances. The type of rod holder depends on what type of rod you use; spinning, baitcasting, and fly-fishing rods are all different types. Spinning and bait casters can usually fit in either rod holder; fly rods, however, will require a different holder due to the setup of the rod and reel.

Investing in quality safety gear is an investment in your well-being on the water. Before each trip, ensure all your safety equipment is in good working order and easily accessible. Remember, conditions on the water can change rapidly, and being prepared with the right gear can make all the difference in ensuring a safe and enjoyable kayak fishing experience. Equip yourself wisely, stay vigilant, and you'll be ready to focus on the excitement kayak fishing offers.

4. Kayak Safety

Tips and Strategies to Remain Safe When Kayaking

Each kayak fishing adventure combines the thrill of the catch with the serenity of nature. However, safety should always be your top concern to ensure each trip is enjoyable and incident-free. Below are essential tips and strategies to help you stay safe while kayak fishing:

Embarking on a kayak fishing adventure is an exciting way to enjoy the great outdoors, but safety should always be your top priority. Here are some crucial tips and strategies to help you stay safe while kayak fishing:

- Always Wear a Personal Flotation Device (PFD): A PFD is essential for your safety on the water. It keeps you afloat in case you capsize or fall overboard. Ensure it fits properly and is comfortable enough to wear at all times.

- Check Weather and Water Conditions Before You Go: Weather can change rapidly, affecting water conditions and your safety. Always check the forecast for wind, rain, storms, and temperature changes. Avoid going out in adverse conditions.

- Inform Someone of Your Float Plan: Let a friend or family member know where you're going, your expected route, and when you plan to return. This information is vital in case of an emergency.

- Carry Essential Safety Equipment: Equip your kayak with safety gear such as a whistle, flashlight, and a first-aid kit. These items can help you signal for help and manage minor injuries.

- Dress Appropriately for the Water Temperature: Hypothermia is a risk even in warm air temperatures if the water is cold. Wear a wetsuit or drysuit when necessary, and dress in layers with moisture-wicking fabrics.

- Practice Self-Rescue Techniques: Learn how to re-enter your kayak from the water. Practice in controlled environments until you're confident in your ability to recover from a capsize. Practicing self-rescue techniques when kayak fishing equips you to quickly and safely re-enter your kayak if you capsize or fall overboard. This preparedness enhances your safety by reducing the risk of hypothermia or drowning and increases your confidence on the water.

- Stay Hydrated and Protect Yourself from the Sun: Bring plenty of water and wear sunscreen, sunglasses, and a hat. Dehydration and sunburn can impair your judgment and physical ability.

- Avoid Alcohol and Drugs: Substance use impairs your coordination, balance, and decision-making skills, increasing the risk of accidents. Avoiding alcohol and drugs while kayak fishing is crucial because these substances impair your judgment, coordination, and reaction time, significantly increasing the risk of accidents or injuries on the water. Staying sober ensures you remain alert and able to make quick, safe decisions, thereby enhancing your safety and the safety of others while kayaking.

- Know Your Physical Limits: Be honest about your fitness level and don't push beyond your capabilities. Fatigue can lead to mistakes and accidents. Failing to do so can lead to fatigue, reduced coordination, and impaired judgment, all of which increase the risk of accidents on the water. By being aware of and respecting your capabilities, you ensure a safe experience, allowing you to respond effectively to challenges and enjoy your time on the kayak without unnecessary risks.

- Keep Your Kayak Visible: Keeping your kayak visible when kayak fishing is essential for your safety because it ensures that other boaters and watercraft operators can see you, reducing the risk of collisions. High visibility, achieved through bright colors, flags, or lights, is especially important in areas with heavy boat traffic or low-light conditions, helping to prevent accidents and keeping you safe on the water.

- Understand Currents and Tides: Be aware of how water movements can affect your kayak. Strong currents and tides can make paddling difficult and dangerous. Understanding currents and tides is crucial when fishing in a kayak because they directly affect your safety by influencing your kayak's movement, stability, and ability to navigate. Being aware of these factors helps you position yourself effectively, avoid hazardous conditions, and optimize your chances of a successful fishing experience.

- Maintain Your Equipment: Regularly inspect your kayak, paddle, and gear for signs of wear or damage. Proper maintenance prevents equipment failure on the water. More on this will be discussed in a later chapter.

- Don't Overload Your Kayak: Exceeding the weight capacity can compromise stability and increase the risk of capsizing. Distributing weight evenly in a kayak is crucial for maintaining stability and balance, which reduces the risk of capsizing and ensures efficient paddling. An even weight distribution allows for better control and maneuverability, enhancing safety and comfort during your kayaking experience.

- Learn Basic Navigation Skills: Understanding how to use a map, compass, or GPS helps prevent you from getting lost, especially in unfamiliar waters. Learning basic navigation skills when fishing in a kayak ensures you can safely navigate waterways, avoid getting lost, and return to your starting point, especially in unfamiliar areas. It also allows you to identify and reach prime fishing spots more effectively, enhancing your overall fishing experience.

- Be Cautious When Anchoring: Only anchor in safe conditions. Avoid anchoring in strong currents, high winds, or deep waters without proper equipment and knowledge. More information on anchoring will be discussed in a later chapter.

- Stay Alert and Aware of Your Surroundings: Be vigilant for obstacles, other vessels, and changes in weather. Awareness helps you react promptly to potential hazards. Staying alert and aware of your surroundings enables you to detect potential hazards like changing weather conditions, approaching boats, or obstacles in the water. This awareness also enhances your fishing experience by allowing you to observe fish activity and environmental cues that can lead to more successful catches.

- Follow Local Laws and Regulations: Adhering to rules regarding fishing licenses, catch limits, and protected areas ensures legal compliance and conservation of resources. Following local laws and regulations ensures you are fishing legally, avoiding fines or legal repercussions. Additionally, these regulations are designed to protect fish populations and aquatic ecosystems, so adhering to them supports conservation efforts and promotes sustainable fishing practices.

- Avoid Standing Unless Your Kayak Is Designed for It: Standing can make the kayak unstable and increase the risk of falling overboard. Only do so if your kayak is built for stand-up fishing. Standing in a kayak that isn't designed for it increases the risk of capsizing due to decreased stability, which can lead to accidents or loss of equipment. Kayaks engineered for standing have enhanced stability features, so only standing in these specially designed kayaks ensures your safety and balance while fishing.

- Avoid Hazardous Areas: Avoid dangerous spots like rapids, weirs, or areas with heavy boat traffic to reduce the risk of accidents. Avoid hazardous areas when fishing in a kayak because such areas can pose significant risks like strong currents, rocks, or submerged obstacles that could capsize your kayak or cause injury. Steering clear of these dangers ensures your safety on the water, allowing you to focus on enjoying your fishing experience without unnecessary risks.

Remember that following these safety tips and strategies will create a secure foundation for your kayak fishing adventures. Preparation and caution not only protect you but also enhance your overall enjoyment on the water. Safe kayaking allows you to focus on the thrill of fishing and the beauty of nature, making each trip a rewarding experience.

Pre-trip planning is crucial for kayak fishing as it ensures your safety and enjoyment on the water. Taking the time to prepare allows you to identify potential hazards, such as changing weather conditions, strong currents, or unfamiliar navigation routes. Planning ahead involves checking the weather forecast, informing someone of your itinerary, inspecting your equipment, and packing essential safety gear. This proactive approach helps you anticipate challenges and make informed decisions, reducing the risk of accidents. Thorough pre-trip planning ensures you're well-prepared to handle whatever the day may bring, allowing you to fish confidently and focus on the adventure ahead.

5. Entering and Exiting Your Kayak

Steps to Safely Enter and Exit Depending on Your Location

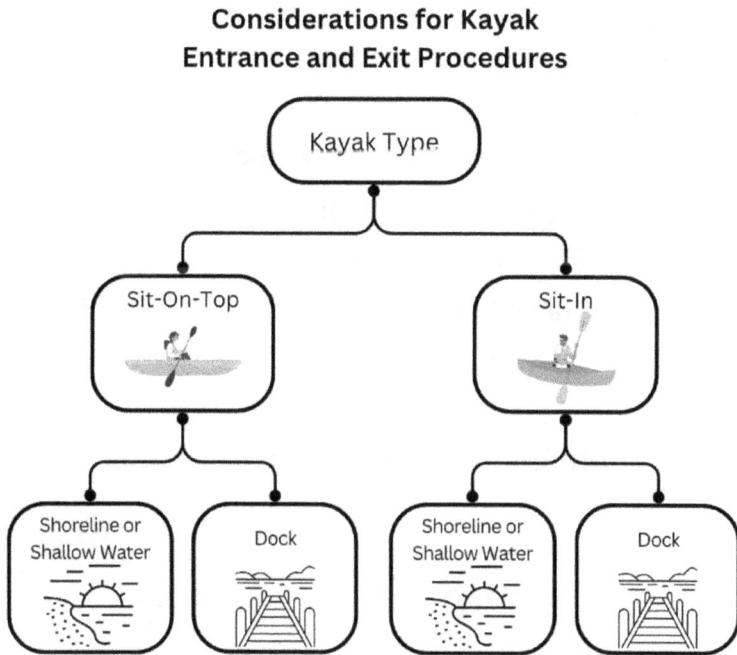

Considerations for Kayak Entrance and Exit Procedures

Kayak Type

Sit-On-Top

Sit-In

Shoreline or Shallow Water

Dock

Shoreline or Shallow Water

Dock

Entering and exiting a kayak can be challenging for beginners, but with the right techniques, it becomes much easier and safer. Whether you're using a sit-in or sit-on-top kayak, the following steps will guide you through the process. We'll also cover considerations for different body types—including adults and kids—to ensure everyone can enjoy kayak fishing confidently. I have also included some online resources to further your learning.

General Tips for Safe Entry and Exit

- Keep Weight Centered: Always aim to keep your body weight over the centerline of the kayak.
- Stay Low: Lower your center of gravity by bending your knees and keeping movements smooth.
- Secure Loose Items: Ensure all gear is stowed or secured to prevent tipping or loss.
- Wear Proper Footwear: Non-slip, water-resistant shoes can improve footing and safety.
- Practice Makes Perfect: Rehearse these techniques in controlled environments before heading out.

Entering and Exiting a Sit-On-Top Kayak

Entering from Shoreline or Shallow Water

1. Position the Kayak: Place the kayak in shallow water, perpendicular to the shore, with the bow (front) pointing away from land.

2. Stabilize the Kayak: Ensure the kayak is steady. You can hold onto the sides or have someone assist you.
3. Sit on the Seat:
   <u>Adults</u>:
   - Stand beside the kayak and face forward.
   - Place one foot in the center of the kayak and lower your backside onto the seat while keeping your weight centered.
   - If you are tall enough, straddle your kayak, positioning yourself above the cockpit, and sit when your body is above the seat.
   <u>Kids</u>:
   - Adults can hold the kayak steady while the child steps into the center and sits down carefully.
4. Bring Your Legs In: Lift your other leg into the kayak, placing your feet on the footrests.
5. Adjust and Push Off: Make sure you're comfortable and use your paddle or hands to push away from the shore.

Exiting to Shoreline or Shallow Water

1. Approach the Shore: Paddle until the kayak bottoms out gently on the shoreline.
2. Prepare to Stand: Place your paddle across the kayak for balance.
3. Swing Legs Over: Turn your body to the side and swing your legs out of the kayak.

4. Stand Up Carefully:
Adults: Push up from the seat, keeping your weight centered, and step onto the ground.
Kids: Help by holding the kayak steady for them as they stand up.

Entering From a Dock

1. Position the Kayak: Place the kayak parallel to the dock, securing it with ropes or have someone hold it steady.
2. Sit On the Dock Edge: Sit down facing the kayak with your feet dangling over the edge.
3. Lower Feet into the Kayak: Place your feet into the footwells of the kayak.
4. Lower Yourself In: Hold onto the dock and carefully lower your body into the seat, keeping weight centered.
5. Push Off: Use your paddle or hands to push away from the dock.

Exiting to a Dock

1. Approach the Dock: Paddle alongside the dock and secure the kayak.
2. Hold the Dock: Grab the dock for stability.

3. Lift Yourself onto the Dock: Shift your weight onto the dock, lifting your body while keeping the kayak steady. Have someone help you if needed.
4. Bring Legs Out: Pull your legs out of the kayak and onto the dock.

Entering and Exiting a Sit-In-Kayak

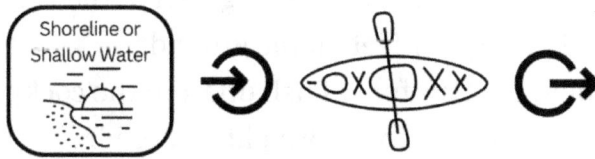

Entering from Shoreline or Shallow Water

1. Position the Kayak: Place the kayak in shallow water with the bow (front) facing out.
2. Stabilize Using Paddle Bride Technique: Place your paddle behind the cockpit, perpendicular to the kayak, with one blade on the shore and the other on the kayak for support.
3. Sit on the Cockpit Edge:
   Adults: Stand over the kayak, facing forward, and lower yourself onto the seat or rear edge of the cockpit.
   Kids: Adults can assist by holding the kayak steady.
4. Bring Legs In: Slide your legs into the cockpit, one at a time, placing feet on the footrests.
5. Adjust Seating: Settle into the seat, ensuring comfort and proper leg positioning.

6. Push Off: Use your paddle to push away from the shore.

Exiting to Shoreline or Shallow Water

1. Approach the Shore: Glide the kayak onto the shore until it stops.
2. Stabilize Using Paddle: Use the paddle bridge technique for support.
3. Bring Legs Out: Lift your legs out of the cockpit and place your feet on the ground.
4. Stand Up Carefully: Push up from the cockpit edge or seat, keeping your weight centered.

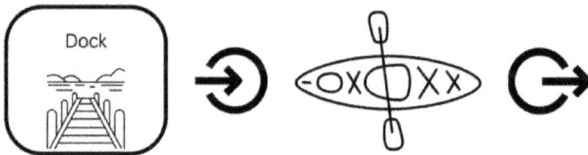

Entering from a Dock

1. Position the Kayak: Align the kayak parallel to the dock.
2. Stabilize the Kayak: Secure the kayak with ropes or have someone hold it.
3. Sit on Dock Edge: Sit facing the kayak with feet over the edge.
4. Lower Legs into Cockpit: Place your feet inside the cockpit onto the footrests.
5. Lower Yourself In: Hold onto the dock and carefully lower into the seat.

6. Push Off: Use your paddle to move away from the dock.

Exiting to a Dock

1. Approach the Dock: Paddle parallel to the dock and secure the kayak.
2. Hold Onto Dock: Grasp the dock for stability.
3. Lift Yourself Out: Shift weight onto the dock and lift your body up.
4. Bring Legs Out: Pull your legs from the cockpit onto the dock.

Tips for Different Body Types and Ages

Adults with Larger Body Types:

- Choose Appropriate Kayaks: Opt for wider kayaks with larger cockpits for better stability and ease of entry/exit.
- Take Your Time: Move slowly and deliberately to maintain balance.
- Use Assistive Techniques: The paddle bridge technique can provide extra support.
- Seek Assistance: Don't hesitate to ask for help.

Kids:

- Supervision is Key: Always assist and supervise children during entry and exit.
- Use Child-Sized Equipment: Smaller kayaks and paddles suited for kids enhance safety and comfort.
- Practice in Calm Conditions: Begin in shallow, calm waters to build confidence.
- Teach Safety Basics: Instruct on proper techniques and the importance of staying centered.

There are many other resources available online. One very useful resource is on the REI website and labeled "How to Launch a Kayak." The site has step by step instruction as well as pictures demonstrating each step.

By following these steps and considering your individual needs, beginners of all ages and body types can confidently and safely enter and exit both sit-in and sit-on-top kayaks. With practice and patience, these techniques will become second nature, enhancing your overall kayak fishing experience.

6. Anchoring

Tips and Methods to Setup Your Kayak to Safely Anchor

Anchoring is a great way to enjoy the scenery or, if you are in a good fishing area, a way to stay there. Anchoring safely depends on the type of bottom at the bottom of the water you are fishing. Many anchor options are commonly used in kayak fishing. The two most common are stake-out-poles and grapnel anchors.

Stake-out-pole

Stake-out-poles are long weighted poles that are thrown into the bottom. These work best in bottoms that are mud, sand, or shallow bodies of water.

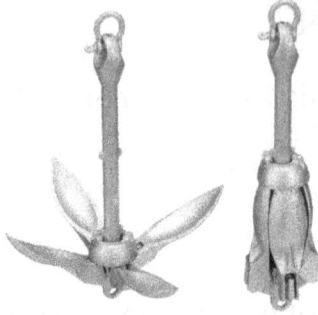

Grapnel Anchor Open and Closed

Grapnel anchors consist of several tines that fold out to grip rocky or weedy bottoms. These are versatile enough for a variety of bottoms and are the most commonly used type of anchor when kayak fishing.

Claw anchors resemble a claw and dig securely into sandy, rocky, or muddy bottoms. These anchors offer a secure hold and can even reset themselves if the current or wind changes direction.

Mushroom anchors are shaped like a mushroom and are best where secure anchoring is required. These anchors are typically the heaviest and bulkiest and are not commonly used in kayak fishing.

Drift Chute

While not necessarily an anchor, drift chutes, or drift socks, allow your speed to be decreased if you are fishing in windy conditions. These act like a parachute and reduce your drift speed.

Typically, I use a kayak grapnel anchor or a stake-out-pole. These are easily stored in my kayak and can be changed depending on the need. There are kayak-specific grapnel anchors that weigh about 3 pounds and come complete with a bag and rope attached. The same is true for stake-out-poles. With the overall low weight of kayaks, I have seen people using a brick, a water bottle filled with sand, or a milk jug filled with gravel. Anchors don't have to be expensive to work. Just be mindful of the bottom of the area where you are fishing. Anchors can get snagged, and extreme pulling on the line can cause your kayak to flip. You should also be aware of the ecosystem that you are fishing, as certain anchors can damage the water bottom. There are also areas where anchoring is prohibited, so be mindful of local regulations and laws.

Rigging an anchor trolley system is a good idea that will allow you to remain in the desired fishing spot while maintaining orientation. They can be added in a few simple steps and are an easy DIY upgrade. This is not something that you need, it is simply a convenience. I have this setup on my kayak, but I often don't use it. Kits are available at large-box sporting goods stores as well as online.

Anchor Trolley Kit

Equipment needed:

- Anchor of choice (about 1.5 to 3.5 pounds)
- Anchor rope (at least 50 feet, depending on water depth)
- Anchor trolley system (optional but recommended)
- Carabiner and/or anchor cleat

- Buoy (optional)
- Cleat (if your kayak doesn't have one already)

Step-by-Step Guide:

Step 1: Install an Anchor Trolley

(Optional but Recommended)

- Mount the Pulleys: Attach one pulley at the bow and one at the stern of your kayak. These should be on the same side of the kayak.
- Run the Rope: Thread a rope through these pulleys. This rope will act as your trolley line.
- Attach a Ring or Carabiner: Secure a ring or carabiner to the middle of the trolley line. This is where you'll attach your anchor rope, allowing you to adjust the anchor point from bow to stern.

Step 2: Prepare the Anchor Line

- Attach Rope to Anchor: Secure one end of your anchor rope to the anchor. Make sure the knot is tight and secure.
- Add a Buoy (Optional): Tie a buoy to the rope. This helps you retrieve the anchor if you need to detach it in an emergency.
- Secure the Other End: Attach the other end of the rope to a carabiner. You can also install an anchor cleat on your kayak to secure the rope.

Step 3: Connect the Anchor Line to the Kayak

- Using the Trolley System: Clip the carabiner with the anchor line to the ring or carabiner on your anchor trolley. This setup allows you to change the anchor point from the front to the back of the kayak, which helps you manage how your kayak faces the current or wind.

- Direct Attachment (Without Trolley): If you don't use a trolley system, you can attach the rope directly to a secure point near the center of the kayak or wherever you find it most stable.

Step 4: Deploying the Anchor

- Check Depth: Ensure your rope is long enough for the depth at which you're anchoring.

- Lower the Anchor: Gently lower the anchor into the water, allowing the rope to uncoil smoothly until it hits the bottom.

- Set the Anchor: Once the anchor touches the bottom, let out a bit more rope (about 1.5 to 2 times the depth) and then secure the rope to your kayak using the cleat or by locking the carabiner.

Step 5: Adjusting Position

- Adjust Trolley: If using a trolley system, you can slide the trolley to adjust the kayak's orientation to face into or away from the wind or current. This is useful for fishing and stability.

Step 6: Retrieving the Anchor

- Pull Up the Rope: When ready to move, pull the rope in, hand-over-hand, until the anchor is visible and free from the bottom. Depending on the bottom, the anchor may be dirty. Shake the anchor off in the water to prevent getting your area dirty before bringing it into your kayak.

- Store Securely: Rinse the anchor, if necessary (to remove mud, weeds, etc.), and secure it along with the rope in a designated storage area on your kayak to prevent it from moving around while paddling.

Anchoring your kayak adds stability and control during your fishing trips, but there are certain conditions and situations where anchoring is not advisable due to safety concerns. Here are some scenarios when it is not safe to anchor a kayak while fishing:

In Fast-Moving Water: Anchoring in fast-moving water, such as in a river with strong currents, can be dangerous. The force of the water can cause the kayak to become unstable, flip over, or even get dragged along, which could lead to accidents or injuries.

In High Wind Conditions: Trying to anchor in high winds can cause the kayak to swing violently or capsize due to the uneven distribution of force on the kayak. High winds can also change direction unexpectedly, complicating the situation further.

In High Traffic Areas: Anchoring in areas with heavy boat traffic, such as channels or marina entrances, can be risky. Other vessels might not see a low-profile kayak, especially if waves or wake obscure it, increasing the risk of collisions.

Near Navigation Channels: Anchoring close to navigation channels with a steady flow of large vessels is dangerous because these boats typically travel at higher speeds and can create large wakes, potentially swamping or overturning your kayak.

In Deep Water Without Proper Equipment: Anchoring in deep water requires specialized equipment to ensure the anchor reaches the bottom and holds securely. Without adequate rope or chain, the anchor may not set properly, leaving the kayak adrift and potentially leading you into unsafe areas.

In Unknown or Rocky Bottoms: Anchoring can be risky if you're unsure about the bottom composition. Sharp rocks or coral can damage the anchor line, and if the anchor gets stuck, it could pose significant challenges and safety risks, especially in adverse conditions.

During Poor Visibility: Fog, heavy rain, or darkness can severely limit visibility. Anchoring in such conditions makes it difficult for other boaters to see you and for you to manage your surroundings effectively.

By understanding and avoiding these unsafe anchoring situations, you'll enhance your safety on the water and ensure a more enjoyable kayak fishing experience. Always prioritize safety over convenience, and don't hesitate to adjust your plans based on the conditions you encounter.

7. Kayak Fishing Techniques

Methods and Strategies to Optimize Kayak Fishing

As I mentioned, fishing from a kayak differs from fishing from a motorized boat. Unless you have great balance, what you can reach from your seated position is what you will reach. I like to keep my equipment in front of me or immediately behind me in a recessed well. My tackle is very contained and downsized, as are my poles. I typically bring three poles and one tackle box with several compartments for fishing lures. I won't get into tackle options, as every region will vary, and each region can be a book by itself. One region can have several types of water that are easily accessible, each requiring a different approach to fishing. This is best completed by visiting your local fishing tackle department, talking to locals in your area, or joining a local kayak fishing club.

Kayak fishing offers a unique blend of excitement and tranquility, allowing anglers to access waters often unreachable by larger boats. For beginners, understanding the techniques and strategies specific to kayak fishing can significantly enhance success and enjoyment on the water. This chapter provides comprehensive tips and methods to optimize your kayak fishing adventures.

Proper paddling techniques and correct kayak positioning are essential to successful kayak fishing. Efficient paddling conserves your energy for longer fishing sessions and allows you to move smoothly and quietly through the water, minimizing disturbances that could scare away fish. Mastering different paddling strokes enhances your ability to navigate various water conditions and maintain control of your kayak. Additionally, strategically positioning your kayak concerning wind, current, and fish habitats improves your casting accuracy and increases your chances of landing a catch. Focusing on these fundamentals sets a strong foundation for a safer and more rewarding kayak fishing experience.

Paddling techniques

- Efficient Stroke: Paddle by rotating your torso rather than just your arms. This conserves energy and increases power.

- Feathering the Paddle: Adjust the paddle blades to reduce wind resistance, making paddling in windy conditions easier.
- Bracing: Learn low and high brace techniques to prevent capsizing when encountering waves or sudden shifts.

Kayak positioning strategies

- Approach Stealthily: Paddle quietly to avoid spooking fish. Slow, smooth strokes minimize noise and disturbance. Allow your kayak to glide to its final spot.
- Use Wind and Current: Position your kayak upwind or up current from your target area, allowing you to drift quietly into position.
- Anchor Wisely: When anchoring (if safe to do so), consider wind and current to keep your kayak oriented correctly for casting. This is when an anchor trolley setup is important.

Casting from a kayak presents unique challenges and opportunities. Several techniques help maximize efficiency and success in various fishing environments. Here are some common casting techniques used in kayak fishing and their reasons for being used. An internet search will yield video tutorials for each one.

The Overhead Cast is the most traditional casting technique. In this technique, the rod is swung overhead to cast the bait or lure toward the target. It is ideal for long-distance casting. It's effective when fishing in open water, where distance and precision are needed to reach fish that are far away or in deeper water. Use shorter rods (6 to 7 feet) to make casting easier from a seated position.

The Sidearm Cast involves swinging the rod horizontally at side level, similar to throwing a Frisbee. It is useful for areas with low overhead clearance, such as under trees or near overhanging branches. It's also a good way to maintain a low profile to avoid scaring fish in clear water.

Flipping is a short-range technique in which the fishing line is pulled out manually, and then the lure is flipped softly into the water. This is done without an actual cast and uses minimal rod movement. This technique is stealthy and allows for precise placement of lures into tight spots, such as between branches, under docks, or into dense cover. It is highly effective in shallow waters or congested areas.

The Backhand Cast involves casting the rod and line over the shoulder opposite to the casting arm, similar to a backhand stroke in tennis. It is advantageous when fishing from a seated position in a kayak because it allows anglers to cast to the opposite side without having to reposition themselves. It's useful for covering more water around the kayak.

Each casting technique offers distinct advantages depending on the fishing situation, such as the type of water body, the presence of obstacles, the fish species targeted, and the level of stealth needed. Mastering multiple casting techniques can significantly enhance an angler's ability to adapt to different scenarios and increase their success rate in kayak fishing.

Implementing various effective fishing techniques while kayak fishing is crucial for maximizing your success and enjoyment on the water.

- Trolling allows you to cover more area by paddling slowly with a lure trailing behind, which is especially useful for targeting active fish over larger expanses. When trolling, rod holders are important to keep your hands free for paddling.
- Drifting enables you to present your bait naturally by letting the wind or current move your kayak, conserving energy and providing a stealthy approach to wary fish.
- Vertical Jigging is effective in deeper waters where you can drop your lure directly over detected fish,

making it ideal when you have a fish finder to locate schools or structures. Sight fishing takes advantage of the kayak's low profile and maneuverability in shallow, clear waters, allowing you to visually locate and cast directly to fish. Polarized sunglasses reduce the glare and improve underwater visibility when sight fishing. By mastering these techniques and adapting them to your kayak's capabilities and the environmental conditions, you can significantly enhance your catch rate and overall fishing experience.

Fly fishing from a kayak requires specific adaptations to manage space efficiently and handle the unique challenges of fly casting and line management on the water. Some key adaptations and considerations exist for a successful kayak fly fishing experience.

- You will want a stable kayak design, as stability is crucial due to the motion of casting and managing the fly rod.
- An open deck layout will provide an area free of obstruction to decrease line snagging.
- An anchor system will allow for precise kayak placement and greater casting accuracy.
- Comfortable seating that is adjustable to allow for a higher vantage point for sight fishing and easier casting.

- Easy access to gear and organized so that it can be quickly reached to prevent scaring fish.

Optimizing your kayak fishing involves mastering your kayak, refining fishing techniques, and adapting to the environment. Applying the strategies outlined in this chapter will enhance your efficiency, increase your catch rate, and deepen your enjoyment of the sport. Every trip is an opportunity to learn and grow as an angler. Embrace the journey, stay safe, and happy fishing!

8. Maintenance, Storage, and Transporting

Guidelines to Keep your Kayak in Optimal Shape

Proper care and maintenance of your fishing kayak are essential to ensure its longevity, performance, and safety on the water. This chapter provides practical tips and strategies for maintaining, storing, and transporting your kayak, helping you keep it in top condition for many future fishing adventures.

Maintenance Tips

Regular Cleaning of your kayak is essential for several important reasons, all of which contribute to the longevity, performance, and safety of your equipment. In addition to these aspects, cleaning after each trip can help prevent the transfer of contaminants and invasive species, which can disrupt local ecosystems and harm native wildlife. Rinse your kayak with fresh water after each use, especially if you've been in salt water. Salt can corrode metal fittings and fasteners over time. Periodically, give your kayak a thorough deep cleaning with mild soap and water. Here are some recommended tasks to extend the life of your kayak and equipment.

Regular Cleaning

- ✓ Rinse After Each Use: Always rinse your kayak with fresh water after every outing, especially if you've been in saltwater or muddy conditions. Salt and debris can corrode metal parts and degrade materials over time.
- ✓ Use Mild Soap: Periodically wash your kayak with mild, non-abrasive soap and a soft sponge to remove grime and algae and prevent mold and mildew growth.
- ✓ Avoid Harsh Chemicals: Do not use bleach or strong solvents, as they can damage the kayak's material and finish.
- ✓ Dry Thoroughly: After cleaning, allow your kayak to air dry completely before storage to prevent mold and mildew.

Inspect for Damage

- ✓ Check the Hull: Before and after each trip, inspect the hull for cracks, deep scratches, or dents. Pay special attention to areas frequently in contact with rocks or rough surfaces.

- ✓ Examine Fittings and Hardware: Ensure all screws, bolts, and rivets are tight and free from corrosion. Look for signs of wear on handles, bungee cords, and hatches.
- ✓ Test Moving Parts: If your kayak has a rudder, pedal drive, or adjustable seat, make sure all moving parts function smoothly. Lubricate them as necessary with manufacturer-recommended products.

Cleaner & UV Protectant

Protect Against UV Damage

- ✓ Apply UV Protectant: Prolonged exposure to sunlight can cause fading and weaken the kayak's material. To shield against sun damage, use a UV protectant spray specifically designed for kayaks.
- ✓ Store Out of Direct Sunlight: When not in use, keep your kayak in a shaded area or use a kayak cover to protect it from harmful UV rays.

Maintenance of Accessories

- ✓ Paddle Care: Rinse your paddle after each use, especially the joints, if it's a two-piece paddle. Check for cracks or chips in the blades and shaft.
- ✓ Rod Holders and Mounts: Regularly check that all attachments are secure and free from rust or damage. Tighten any loose fittings.

Preventing Mold and Mildew

- ✓ Ventilation: Open all hatches and compartments during drying to allow air circulation. Moisture trapped inside can lead to mold growth.
- ✓ Storage Position: Store your kayak in a way that allows water to drain naturally to prevent pooling.

Repairing Minor Damage

- ✓ Scratches and Gouges: Small scratches are common and usually don't affect performance. For deeper gouges, use a kayak repair kit or appropriate plastic welding tools.
- ✓ Leaks: If you suspect a leak, perform a float test by filling the kayak with water on land to identify the source. Patch leaks promptly using materials compatible with your kayak's construction.

At the end of your paddling season, perform a detailed inspection and maintenance check. Repair any damage and replace worn parts. Check and tighten all hardware fittings, as these can loosen over time due to regular use and replace any that need replacing. Apply a rubber or plastic conditioner to hatch covers and other rubber components to keep them supple and prevent cracking.

Kayaking involves exposure to a variety of environmental conditions and physical stresses, which can lead to several common types of damage. Identifying and addressing these damages promptly can help maintain your kayak's performance and longevity. Here are some common kayak damages and tips on how to identify them.

Scratches and abrasions are the most common types of damage and are usually visible on the hull. They occur from contact with rocks, gravel, or other rough surfaces. Minor scratches are generally superficial and won't affect the kayak's performance, but deep scratches can weaken the structure and should be repaired. These can often be smoothed or filled with a plastic welder or specific kayak repair kits. Frequently, a razor blade can be used to remove the damaged material, making the area smooth again.

UV Damage is most easily identified by looking for signs of fading color and brittle or chalky surfaces on the kayak's hull. UV damage can weaken the plastic, making it more susceptible to cracking. Regular application of UV protectants can help mitigate this.

Cracks occur in areas under stress, such as around the cockpit or the bottom of the hull. Cracks might also appear near fittings or attachments. Cracks can lead to water leakage and structural failure if not repaired. They should be addressed immediately, often requiring plastic welding or a kayak repair kit. Frequently, these require the assistance of a professional. However, there are kits that can be purchased to complete this task at home.

Dents are usually found on the bottom of the kayak and can be spotted by examining the hull's shape. They can occur from impacts with hard objects or improper storage. Most dents will pop out if left in the sun (as the heat helps the plastic regain its original shape), but persistent dents might affect the kayak's performance and should be addressed.

A visual inspection can identify hardware issues, loose or corroded fittings, rivets and bolts, and increased movement or noise. Loose or damaged hardware can lead to the failure of attached components like seats, foot pegs, or storage hatches and should be tightened or replaced.

Damaged seals and gaskets around storage compartments and the cockpit. Look for cracks, tears, or general wear. Damaged seals can allow water to enter storage areas or the hull, which can be problematic, especially in colder conditions.

Regular maintenance checks and timely resolution of issues can significantly extend the life and performance of your kayak. Following these guidelines will help keep your kayak in optimal condition, ensuring many years of safe and enjoyable use.

Storage Strategies

Proper storage is crucial to maintaining your kayak's shape and integrity during periods of non-use.

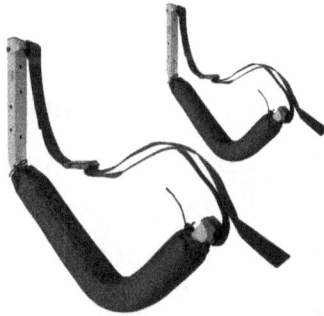

Wall Mounted Storage Rack

1. Indoor Storage

- Ideal Conditions: Storing your kayak indoors is ideal as it protects it from weather elements and temperature extremes.
- Use Racks or Slings: To prevent warping or deformation, support the kayak evenly using wall-mounted racks, ceiling hoists, or padded stands.

- Positioning: Store the kayak on its side or upside down (hull up) to distribute weight evenly and avoid pressure points that can cause dents.

2. Outdoor Storage

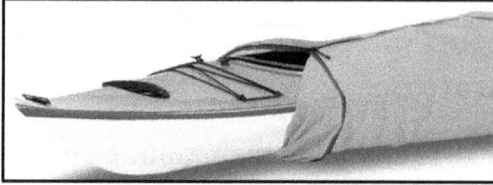

Outdoor Kayak Storage Bag

- Cover Your Kayak: Use a weather-resistant cover to shield your kayak from rain, sun, and debris.
- Elevate Off the Ground: To prevent moisture absorption and discourage pests, keep your kayak off the ground using sawhorses or a dedicated kayak rack.
- Secure Location: Choose a safe area protected from falling branches or heavy snow loads. Use locks to prevent theft.

3. Avoid Extreme Temperatures

- Heat Exposure: High temperatures can cause the kayak's material to warp or become brittle. Avoid storing in direct sunlight or near heat sources.
- Cold Conditions: Freezing temperatures can also make plastic brittle. If possible, store your kayak in a temperature-controlled environment.

4. Protecting from Pests

- Seal Openings: Securely close all hatches and cockpit covers to prevent animals from nesting inside.

- Regular Checks: Inspect your kayak periodically for signs of insects or rodents, especially if stored outdoors.

Transporting Your Kayak

Safely transporting your kayak and fishing gear to and from locations is crucial to ensuring its longevity and functionality when you reach your destination. Here are some essential tips for safely transporting your gear, along with explanations of why each is important.

1. Choosing the Right Transport System

- Roof Racks: Invest in a quality roof rack system designed for kayaks. Options include J-cradles, saddles, or foam blocks, depending on your vehicle and kayak. Research the best option for your vehicle, kayak, and personal ability to load/unload your kayak, as there are many options available depending on your vehicle.

- Trailers: For heavier kayaks or multiple boats, a kayak trailer might be more convenient and easier to load.

- Pickup Trucks: Use a bed extender or secure the kayak diagonally in the bed with appropriate padding and tie-downs.

2. Proper Loading Techniques

- Get Assistance: Whenever possible, have someone help you load and unload to prevent personal injury and damage to your kayak or vehicle.

Thule Hullivator and Yakima HandRoll Kayak Roller

- Use Load Assist Devices: Consider using loading aids like rollers or lift systems if loading solo.
- Protect Your Vehicle and Kayak: Use padding where the kayak contacts the rack or vehicle to prevent scratches and dents.

3. Securing the Kayak

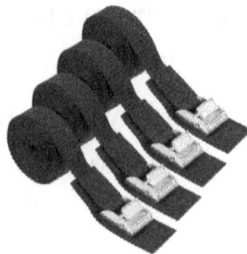

Cam Buckle Tie Down

- Tie-Down Straps: Use cam buckle straps designed for kayaks to secure the kayak firmly to the rack. Avoid the use of ratchet straps as they can easily deform or break your kayak when securing due to over-ratcheting.

Bow and Stern Car Tiedown System

- Bow and Stern Lines: Always attach bow and stern tie-downs to prevent the kayak from shifting or lifting during transit. Failure to do so can cause liability issues to you if your kayak causes an accident or injury to another person or vehicle.

- Check for Movement: After securing, shake the kayak to ensure its stable. Re-check the straps after driving a short distance. Often, the wind and vibration of the vehicle will cause the kayak to settle or shift, resulting in a kayak that is not securely secured.

4. Legal and Safety Considerations

- Overhang Regulations: Be aware of local laws regarding how far items can extend from your vehicle. Attach a red flag to the kayak's end if it extends beyond your car's rear.
- Visibility: Ensure the kayak doesn't obstruct your view or your vehicle lights. Adjust mirrors as needed for safe driving. If your kayak extends beyond your vision, consider purchasing mirror extenders to provide a better field of view.

5. Travel Precautions

- Monitor Weather Conditions: High winds can affect vehicle handling when transporting a kayak on the roof. Drive cautiously in adverse conditions.
- Regular Stops: On long trips, stop periodically to check that the kayak remains secure, and the straps are tight.

6. Unloading Safely

- Choose a Safe Spot: Park in an area clear of traffic and obstacles.
- Use Proper Lifting Techniques: Bend your knees and keep your back straight to prevent injury. Use teamwork when possible.
- Inspect After Transport: Once unloaded, check your kayak for any signs of stress or damage incurred during transport.

Additional Tips

Kayak Cart

Use a kayak cart for ground transport to minimize the physical effort needed to transport your kayak from your vehicle to the water, reducing the risk of dropping it or banging it against hard surfaces. It also helps handle the kayak over rough terrains, protecting the hull from abrasions. It is generally advised to avoid kayak carts where the cart extends through the scupper holes. The scupper hole type of cart can weaken the scupper hole in the boat, causing damage to the hull and allowing water to enter if a crack forms. They are generally more difficult to load than a traditional sit-on-top kayak cart.

Use padded cases or rod sleeves to protect against scratches, dents, and more severe structural damage from accidental drops or impacts against hard surfaces. Secure loose items that can get lost or cause damage if they move around during transport. Secure all small items like lures, hooks, and other tackle in closed and latched boxes. This prevents them from scattering or getting damaged and ensures that sharp objects are safely contained.

Organize your gear efficiently to save time and prevent damage caused by improper packing. Use dividers or separate containers within larger storage boxes to keep gear from colliding.

Cover gear during transport using a tarp or specialized cover for gear on roof racks to protect against environmental elements like sun, rain, and road debris during transport. This helps prevent UV damage, water ingress, and physical impacts from airborne debris.

Regularly inspect transport equipment such as racks, straps, and trailers to ensure they remain in good condition and function correctly. Worn straps or faulty rack systems can fail, leading to gear loss or damage.

Keep records of your kayak's serial number, purchase date, and warranties. This information is valuable for insurance claims or repairs if they are needed.

Taking the time to properly maintain, store, and transport your fishing kayak ensures it's always ready for your next adventure. Regular care extends the life of your kayak and enhances safety and performance on the water. By following these guidelines, you'll protect your investment and enjoy many successful and enjoyable fishing trips for many years.

9. Photographing Your Catch

Tips and Strategies for Photographing Your Catch

Photographing your catch is a rewarding way to preserve the memories of your kayak fishing adventures. However, taking great photos from a kayak presents unique challenges due to limited space, water movement, and the need to handle fish carefully. This chapter provides essential tips and strategies to help you capture stunning images of your catch while ensuring the safety and well-being of both you and the fish

- Prepare your camera in advance by having your camera or smartphone ready and easily accessible before you even start fishing. This means setting the camera on a quick-access mode, like sports or action settings, which are ideal for quick shots. Ensuring everything is set up in advance minimizes the time the fish spends out of water. Consider using burst mode, if available, to take multiple pictures quickly, increasing the chance of getting the perfect shot.

Chest Harness for Camera

- Use a hands-free setup by mounting an action camera on your kayak or using a chest harness or head mount. Hands-free options allow you to keep handling the fish safely while taking a photo, reducing drop risks and stress on the fish. There are a variety of options available depending on your kayak setup. Some can be mounted to rails; others can be wrapped around an anchor point. Research and find the best option for your kayak setup, photography style, and fishing needs.

- Keep the fish in water while preparing to take the photo. This reduces the stress on the fish and avoids air exposure. Avoid causing unnecessary stress to the fish for the sake of a picture.

- Take photos of the fish partially submerged or at the water's surface, if possible, to minimize stress and potential harm to the fish by reducing air exposure which increases its chances of survival after release. This also captures the fish in its natural environment, resulting in a more authentic and respectful image.

- Limit the time spent handling and photographing the fish to under 30 seconds. Prolonged exposure to air can significantly reduce the fish's chances of survival once released. A simple tip to follow to practice this is to hold your breath while you have the fish out of the water. If you need to take a breath, chances are it's time to get the fish in the water.

- Proper support is essential. If you need to lift the fish, always use both hands. Support the fish horizontally-one hand under the belly, the other near the tail. This helps prevent internal injuries by distributing the fish's weight evenly.

- Avoid touching gills and eyes as they are both extremely sensitive. Avoid touching these areas to prevent unnecessary stress or injury to the fish.

- Use a wide lens. Using a camera or an adjustable smartphone, a wide lens can capture the entire scene without lifting the fish too high or handling it too much. This allows for a quick and safe snapshot with minimal disturbance.

- Before landing the fish, plan your shot by thinking about the type of photo you want. Whether you want a close-up, a full body shot, or a release shot, planning helps reduce the time spent fumbling with the camera during critical moments.

- After taking the picture, practice good fish revival techniques. If the fish shows signs of exhaustion, take a moment to revive it. Hold it gently in the water, moving it back and forth to facilitate water flow through the gills until it swims away strongly. If there is a current face the fish toward the current to give it a rush of oxygenated water. Do not let the fish go until you can feel it begin to swim away on its own.

Following these tips and strategies, you can capture memorable photographs of your catch. Remember that the well-being of the fish and your safety are important. With preparation and practice, you can take stunning photos that preserve the thrill of your fishing adventures for years to come.

10. Being an Ethical Angler

Tips and Strategies to Protect the Wildlife

Kayak fishing offers a unique opportunity to connect intimately with nature, but with this privilege comes the responsibility to protect and preserve the aquatic environments and wildlife we cherish. Being an ethical angler means adopting practices that minimize your impact on the ecosystem, ensure the sustainability of fish populations, and respect the natural habitats of all wildlife. Below are essential tips and strategies to help you become a more responsible and ethical kayak angler.

Follow local fishing regulations by obtaining the proper license and permits for your area. These licenses and permits fund conservation efforts and ensure fishing activities are monitored and regulated. Be sure to carry any required license and/or permits for the area you are fishing. Failure to do so can result in fines.

Be aware of and follow catch limits and size regulations. These regulations relate to quantity and minimum and maximum size of the fish, to maintain healthy fish populations. Ensure you are familiar with the local regulations for each species, and that you are using an accurate measuring device to ensure compliance.

In addition to catch limits and size regulations, it is important to monitor seasonal closures for the area you are fishing. Certain areas or even certain species may be protected during certain times of the year, often during breeding season. These closures allow for adequate time for breeding to ensure the population can replenish in the area.

Proper handling of the fish is crucial to ensuring the fish's survival after catch and release. Employing techniques that minimize stress and injury to the fish contributes to conservation efforts and maintains healthy fish populations for future generations of anglers. Here are some effective techniques for handling fish.

- Wet your hands before handling fish to help protect their slime coat. The slime coat is a protective layer that helps prevent infections and injuries from parasites and bacteria. Dry hands can remove this slime, exposing the fish to potential health issues.

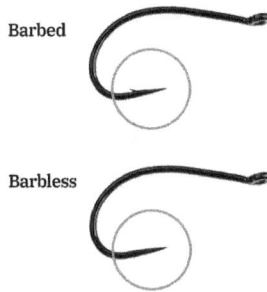

Barbed and Barbless Hooks

- Use barbless hooks or crush the barbs because they cause less damage to the fish's mouth, and they are much easier and quicker to remove. This reduces the handling time and stress experienced by the fish, enhancing their survival after release.

- Keep the fish in water as much as possible to maintain their gill function and reduce stress. Air exposure should be minimized as even a few seconds out of water can significantly impact a fish's survival chances.

How to Support a Fish

How to Support a Fish

- Use proper support when handling large fish. Supporting the belly of larger fish when lifting them can prevent internal injuries. Large fish are not designed to support their own weight out of water, which can damage their internal organs if they are hung vertically by the mouth. Holding a fish by the mouth only can cause damage to its mouth, even breaking the mouth or jaw.

- Use rubberized nets instead of nylon or knotted nets. Rubberized nets are gentler on the fish's skin, fins, and slime coat. Nylon or knotted nets can cause more physical damage and remove more of the protective slime coat.

- For heavy fish, avoid using a grip tool on the jaw. Grip tools can dislocate or break the jaws of heavier fish, especially if the fish is held vertically. If a grip tool must be used, support the weight of the fish with a second hand under the belly.

- Remove hooks quickly and gently to reduce the duration of stress and physical damage to the fish. Use needle-nose pliers or a hook removal tool to remove the hook efficiently without excessive tugging. If deep hooked, cut the line. If a fish is deep hooked (hooked in the gullet or stomach), it's better to cut the line as close to the hook as possible rather than trying to remove the hook.

Most fish can survive with a hook left in, and it will often dissolve or be expelled over time.

- Revive fish before releasing. Gently hold the fish upright in the water and move it back and forth to facilitate water flow over the gills. This helps the fish regain its strength and oxygen levels before swimming away, increasing its chances of survival.

Prevent the spread of invasive species by cleaning your kayak and gear following each fishing trip. Thoroughly washing your kayak, paddles, and any related gear when moving between bodies of water will prevent any invasive species (plant or animal) from being moved to a new body of water. Failure to do so can disrupt or collapse local ecosystems.

Being an ethical angler is about more than just following the rules; it's a commitment to stewardship of the natural world. By adopting these tips and strategies, you contribute to the sustainability of fish populations and the health of aquatic ecosystems. Your actions help ensure that future generations can enjoy the thrill of kayak fishing in pristine environments. Remember, every small effort counts, and together, we can significantly impact preserving the wildlife and waters we love.

11. Leave No Trace

Tips and Strategies to Protect the Environment

The Leave No Trace principles are designed to minimize human impact on the environment, and applying these principles specifically to kayak fishing is essential to protect and preserve natural waterways. I encourage you to further educate yourself on the Leave No Trace principle by visiting *lnd.org*. Here, you can find ways to further protect the environment when exploring the outdoors, not just on the water. Below is a quick list of how to integrate Leave No Trace ethics into your kayak fishing practices.

- ✓ Plan ahead and prepare. Research the area you plan to visit. Know the regulations and special concerns for it, such as fishing limits, size regulations, protected species, and sensitive habitats.
- ✓ Avoid high-use times to minimize the impact on natural resources and wildlife.

- ✓ Understanding local regulations and environmental concerns helps you avoid causing unintended damage to ecosystems.
- ✓ Travel and fish on durable surfaces by using established launching and landing sites to access waterways. Launch your kayak from designated areas to prevent erosion and damage to shoreline vegetation. Avoid banks with fragile plants or nesting sites.
- ✓ When choosing spots to fish, stay within the confines of deep water as much as possible, avoiding fragile shallow areas where boat and paddle contact can damage the bottom habitat. Reducing disturbance to the shoreline and riverbed protects aquatic habitats and maintains water quality.
- ✓ Dispose of waste properly. Carry out all trash, including fishing line, bait containers, and food wrappers. Be mindful of human waste regulations in the area; use facilities or carry a portable waste disposal system if required. Waste left behind can harm wildlife, pollute waterways, and degrade the natural beauty of fishing spots.
- ✓ Observe but do not disturb wildlife and aquatic habitats. Avoid introducing or transporting non-native species (this includes releasing unused bait) by cleaning your gear thoroughly between trips, including your kayak, fishing gear, and boots.

Preserving natural conditions ensures that ecosystems remain vibrant and diverse for future generations.

✓ Observe wildlife from a distance and do not follow or approach them. Be particularly careful not to disrupt nesting birds or spawning fish. Disturbing wildlife can stress animals, leading to harmful behavioral changes and affecting their survival.

✓ Be considerate of other visitors. Respect other users of the waterways. Keep noise levels down and maintain a low profile when fishing near others to avoid disrupting their experience.

Sharing natural spaces respectfully ensures that everyone can enjoy their recreational activities without being impacted by others. By adhering to these Leave No Trace principles, kayak anglers can help protect waterways' natural beauty and integrity, ensuring these resources remain vibrant and accessible for future generations.

12. Next Steps

Next Steps for Your Kayak Fishing Journey

Congratulations on taking the first steps into the exciting world of kayak fishing. As you continue to develop your skills and confidence on the water, there are numerous ways to enhance your experience and deepen your connection with this rewarding sport. Here are some next steps to consider as you embark on your ongoing kayak fishing journey:

Practice and Refine Your Paddling Techniques: Efficient paddling conserves energy, increases your range, and improves maneuverability on the water. Dedicate time to practice different strokes and maneuvers. Consider taking a paddling course to learn from professionals.

Enhance Your Fishing Skills: Developing various fishing techniques will make you a more versatile and successful angler. Experiment with new lures, baits, and fishing methods like trolling, jigging, or fly fishing from your kayak.

Join Local Kayak Fishing Clubs or Online Communities: Connecting with other kayak anglers offers opportunities for camaraderie, knowledge exchange, and group outings.

Participate in forums, social media groups, or local clubs to share experiences and learn from others.

Explore New Fishing Locations: Trying different waterways exposes you to new challenges and fish species, enhancing your skills and enjoyment. Research and plan trips to nearby lakes, rivers, or coastal areas you've never fished.

Invest in Advanced Gear and Accessories: Upgrading equipment can improve comfort, efficiency, and success rates. Consider adding items like a fish finder, GPS, upgraded rod holders, or a more comfortable seat to your kayak setup.

Learn About Local Fish Species and Habitats: Understanding fish behavior and ecosystems increases your chances of a successful catch. Study the feeding patterns, preferred habitats, and seasonal movements of target species in your area.

Engage in Conservation Efforts: Protecting waterways ensures the longevity of the sport and the health of aquatic ecosystems. Participate in cleanup events, practice catch and release when appropriate, and advocate for sustainable fishing practices.

Stay Updated on Regulations and Best Practices: Compliance with laws ensures sustainable fishing and avoids legal issues. Regularly check for updates on fishing regulations, license requirements, and protected areas.

Reflect on Your Experiences: Reflection helps you learn from successes and mistakes, fostering continuous improvement. After each trip, note what worked well and areas for improvement in your techniques or gear setup.

Keep the Fun in Fishing: Remembering why you started kayak fishing keeps the passion alive. Focus on enjoyment, whether it's the tranquility of nature, the thrill of the catch, or the joy of adventure.

As you take these next steps, remember that kayak fishing is a journey of continuous learning and enjoyment. Each outing is an opportunity to grow as an angler and to deepen your appreciation for the natural world. Stay curious, stay safe, and most importantly, have fun out there!

Conclusion and Thank You

For many, myself included, kayak fishing is more than a hobby, rather it's a doorway to experiences that refresh the soul. The serenity of gliding over calm waters, the thrill of the catch, and the profound connection with nature are moments that leave lasting impressions. This sport also provides a wonderful form of low-impact exercise that can improve your physical health and offers an intimate connection with nature that rejuvenates the spirit. Every outing is an opportunity to learn something new, not just about fishing techniques or aquatic environments, but about yourself. I recommend embracing each moment—the quiet mornings, the unexpected catches, even the days when the fish are elusive—as they all contribute to the creation of your personal fishing story.

As you continue your kayak fishing journey, I challenge you to stay curious, remain respectful of the natural world, and perhaps most importantly, share your experiences. Whether teaching a friend, participating in conservation efforts, or simply telling your tales around a campfire or relaxed dinner, your passion can inspire others to discover the wonders of kayak fishing. Your contributions are valuable, and together, we can build a vibrant and supportive network of kayak anglers united by our passion for casting lines in the quiet corners of the world.

As we reach the end of this journey together, I want to thank you once again for choosing this book to be part of your initiation into this incredible sport that I have enjoyed for over 20 years. I hope you feel equipped with the knowledge and confidence to explore these waters safely and responsibly. May your adventures be plentiful, your catches memorable, and your spirit ever adventurous. Safe paddling and happy fishing!

Author kayaking on an urban lake

References

Amazon.Com: 2 Pcs Quick Hood Loop Tie Down Anchor Straps & 2 Pcs Heavy Duty Ratchet Tie Down Straps,Adjustable Pulley Rope Hanger with Reinforced Metal Gear,Quick Hood Loop Anchor Straps for Car,Kayak,Truck,Canoe : Sports & Outdoors. https://www.amazon.com/dp/B0D5QG9RN3/ref=sspa_dk_detail_8?psc=1&pd_rd_i=B0D5QG9RN3&pd_rd_w=jauKn&content-id=amzn1.sym.f2f1cf8f-cab4-44dc-82ba-0ca811fb90cc&pf_rd_p=f2f1cf8f-cab4-44dc-82ba-0ca811fb90cc&pf_rd_r=9CKTSVK9059H2F46VN4J&pd_rd_wg=0BRjR&pd_rd_r=83457544-ba41-4f7d-9b13-ffc4b115640b&s=automotive&sp_csd=d2lkZ2V0TmFtZT1zcF9kZXRhaWxfdGhlbWF0aWM. Accessed 12 Oct. 2024.

Amazon.Com : Amazon Basics Adjustable Chest Mount Harness for GoPro Camera (Compatible with GoPro Hero Series), Black : Electronics. https://www.amazon.com/AmazonBasics-Chest-Mount-Harness-cameras/dp/B01D3I8A7A/ref=sr_1_1_ffob_sspa?crid=3HBDMT5DQNVWM&dib=eyJ2IjoiMSJ9.Abtd2PHw1Y26vAyBIo1U6lSZeYuWSSLgorjLLKBe9P85rwlze6jXECjmfheJmYmaeNc6kDEc7d2sEOSmgDpn5BQ5Q5-krcrZMQCndSlEtLNrQcaHoJgi23E_xal0thYbCgQ_w3SkSjyHbDEAZaHLFSajqOuHKB5KhukcBDjWTI47H02o33iZWFcbVRQbqT0rlou9ASMN_IHoObPY_Tf2KqLk90hvqpHCfOZLVVcBzU.Hgm7ziykM2JDOG2vq0H63sZH8aLmOg0rCdpWjrHVB0&dib_tag=se&keywords=chest%2Bstrap%2Bfor%2Bcamera&qid=1728093886&sprefix=chest%2Bstrap%2Bfor%2B%2Caps%2C217&sr=8-1-

spons&sp_csd=d2lkZ2V0TmFtZT1zcF9hdGY&th=1.
Accessed 12 Oct. 2024.

Amazon.Com: Axlksia 8 Pcs Kayak Scupper Plugs Kit, Silicone Universal Kayak Scupper Plug Drain Holes Stopper Bung with Lanyard, Kayak Accessories : Sports & Outdoors.
https://www.amazon.com/Axlksia-Scupper-Silicone-Universal-Accessories/dp/B0CFRL4LP9/ref=sxin_16_pa_sp_search_thematic_sspa?content-id=amzn1.sym.aa47d3ff-52c9-4381-95f2-032c3090aaca%3Aamzn1.sym.aa47d3ff-52c9-4381-95f2-032c3090aaca&cv_ct_cx=scupper+plugs&dib=eyJ2IjoiMSJ9.u1EjAQ_5RxLIj5XFC8IlsLGDUHBO1zqI7tZk1CuQ4SeHg5QnM-EbqYdPVqkc1GTmoV1AgcwKnv5b_NkDK_2Sw9ku5UDKbJUTpZ1sZFsC3PE.25AY_Grm0MDJgJG2OFglYqzFdD5V8xR1qes1Ck1IpiM&dib_tag=se&keywords=scupper+plugs&pd_rd_i=B0CFRL4LP9&pd_rd_r=e3c7e95b-f1d1-4f2f-8563-081407ca3677&pd_rd_w=jItKt&pd_rd_wg=4rxY8&pf_rd_p=aa47d3ff-52c9-4381-95f2-032c3090aaca&pf_rd_r=Y645TYVQ0EQZDGTPEDP7&qid=1728004698&sbo=RZvfv%2F%2FHxDF%2BO5021pAnSA%3D%3D&sr=1-1-9428117c-b940-4daa-97e9-ad363ada7940-spons&sp_csd=d2lkZ2V0TmFtZT1zcF9zZWFyY2hfdGhlbWF0aWM&psc=1. Accessed 12 Oct. 2024.

Amazon.Com: Ayaport Cam Buckle Tie Down Straps Lashing Straps 2200lbs Break Strength Heavy Duty Car Roof Rack Strap for Kayak, SUP, Surfboard, Cargo, Motorcycle, Truck, Boat, Dirt Bike (1" x 8') : Sports & Outdoors.
https://www.amazon.com/Ayaport-Lashing-Strength-Surfboard-

Motorcycle/dp/B09YHD2RXJ/ref=sr_1_19_sspa?crid=1FT
7Q3KU4JQJX&dib=eyJ2IjoiMSJ9.tc26yqku39TvjHmDs_G
ZkYcXTDO-
O8Hx7xBqso9mRI_IO2bAS4lBT9OknXHIvfOsgeYbvJ-
QNG358dkQnzNuS2jWmUw5VSmIWPtnDKdTh8ZCKY8ggI
QztFE0zv5CR0gAHOBgwrygPhAp0nyjV-
Nf29VCx17l76P9fNHdJuWrTsfGfUzUde1sg5qL_yFy-
aGSPPy-
Lg0QtTHYHV0MM3ED9Ql9ndtLAmTsuxGM3EaHxQTaGw
Xk2U82fCfgupK4HMNHfrXUQEkIc1LeLMIEzXG19yQZKb
megqGVVrJm6qX0L9M.uszEmcEIBmrAIWOD8wpGckkFIJ
GdbJ-
oYu0nrt1eZxM&dib_tag=se&keywords=car%2Btransport%2
Bsystem%2Bfor%2Bkayak%2Btie%2Bdowns&qid=17280951
87&sprefix=car%2Btransport%2Bsystem%2Bfor%2Bkayak%
2Btie%2Bdowns%2Caps%2C276&sr=8-19-
spons&sp_csd=d2lkZ2V0TmFtZT1zcF9tdGGY&th=1.
Accessed 12 Oct. 2024.

*Amazon.Com: Bonnlo Universal Kayak Carrier - Trolley for
Carrying Kayaks, Canoes, Paddleboards, Float Mats, and
Jon Boats - Inflation-Free Solid Tires Wheel 2 Ratchet
Straps : Sports & Outdoors.*
https://www.amazon.com/Bonnlo-Carrier-Trolley-NO-
FLAT-
Transport/dp/B071G5BRYF/ref=sr_1_6?crid=30D5IZ472
WFUT&dib=eyJ2IjoiMSJ9.myqz-
K8wpbNlgXVOexr7LnIE8h9q7OgucaG8AbUEIxbs7S8dUfe_
YfD_Sgj_x79igtc3DuSgY_LX3rTBgsm9D6ZboDzJisGbH7G
x1675FPWqKUrZJFxmqK8NnlFg15X9zI0kKbzEZ_VuTlCvp
rmZ0hoxv-
x_0U1pQ86gVTzBXWk6DbPms6LtHX66OWBlzrk2PoWMp

EXrdTQR3ijf5H5FOYnhQwrutx-kB8y40jgFxYZN98MWY4NtOhMz9wMY0vM-ANz6-xtTamWg3jwRA3KmvvQX9c3bJEiiKdPkBvMMTEM.9LlP-5TeiNS_thqJYPH5CFKBYXtsSEYJR7MDopT9eYo&dib_tag=se&keywords=kayak%2Bcart&qid=1728093809&sprefix=kayak%2Bcart%2Caps%2C235&sr=8-6&th=1. Accessed 12 Oct. 2024.

Amazon.Com: EliteShield Canoe Cover Kayak Cover; Waterproof UV Resistant Marine Grade Polyester Canoe Kayak Boat Storage Cover Fits 15 Ft-16 Ft Long, 116 Inches Girth Gray Color : Sports & Outdoors. https://www.amazon.com/EliteShield-Canoe-Kayak-Waterproof-Weather/dp/B08ZHBBV7R/ref=sr_1_2_sspa?crid=2BZJ1A88U45O6&dib=eyJ2IjoiMSJ9.oN2PFq6Gh_gPzfg-lK7tNNscQ9QIKODlC1817Vjmi3NXDeWLKvuqLzsaB_UQDFpHzFjKTlhLSEkTa75bC8Yhmy4wiBFKd0OtaBTP-W1ODfUiPguvzm73txz-WHGRMTwoi0mM95m2--zN6lzk3BuB59tIakEBad7ThK92wpIRm6LZhOdVaoHvEh-dCVxtrSUAzhS7BzcU6MjehcBEL143iTc8zJ8HpzfcUMTqFV2t89HdKl_sAGcbxBUEU5bwpswGURuZhbnYyZ_h9SaT9FV7LRndtj2oZnkFCo4569O3zPo.IbBbU54L_ZGQk6J_iDRSghAagzayw018kJGaIE9hjys&dib_tag=se&keywords=kayak+cover+for+outdoor+storage&qid=1728095002&sprefix=kayak+storage+cover+out%2Caps%2C212&sr=8-2-spons&sp_csd=d2lkZ2V0TmFtZT1zcF9hdGY&psc=1. Accessed 12 Oct. 2024.

Amazon.Com: Jiozermi 4 Pcs Kayak Scupper Plug, Rubber Drain Holes Stopper Bung, Kayak Drain Plug for Kayak Canoe Boat : Sports & Outdoors. https://www.amazon.com/Jiozermi-Kayak-Scupper-

Rubber-Stopper/dp/B09F36TJ67/ref=sr_1_22_sspa?dib=eyJ2Ijoi MSJ9.xotDsaoAulliGb8q8ku62lKx7ZOJBJ9QK-J4j9geD_DziAvf1tNDLwZmMnm7pqwSZi2AghEX1iZBsyky AV58u-dlEy3O9jSvl2v7gk-a5izoQd4sKtPe48aMkd1dquHQRm2wlOqw_Ux0l0GF3o3d2 4UC-TV_0InoBDv5n_kyEWviFtIIR0ZD75o1fi8WcBYtQtnZiJAU um1EKI6dHn5Foy--0h-dal8-e2Mt3RpRXQ9CKbqPnxText2jHggn2iT2fX9F-E3mtm8Dko_YHL6OzrlefdZxv0EMEeSfmonegzo.aPIOTDE Bp3lrXyotITlIZp-nuncsgdbc99_lSG4iEao&dib_tag=se&keywords=scupper%2 Bplugs&qid=1728004698&sr=8-22-spons&sp_csd=d2lkZ2V0TmFtZT1zcF9tdGY&th=1. Accessed 12 Oct. 2024.

Amazon.Com: Kayak Fishing Rod Holder, Borogo 2 Pack Kayak Deck Flush Mount Fishing Boat Rod Holders and Cap Cover for Kayak, Fishing Boat, Canoe and Fishing Tackle Accessory Tool : Sports & Outdoors. https://www.amazon.com/dp/B0894Q6TBY/ref=sspa_dk_detail_3?psc=1&pd_rd_i=B0894Q6TBY&pd_rd_w=4xmte& content-id=amzn1.sym.386c274b-4bfe-4421-9052-a1a56db557ab&pf_rd_p=386c274b-4bfe-4421-9052-a1a56db557ab&pf_rd_r=RZ2TF0P9Y6W3WDC6EF6Q&pd _rd_wg=wAHcl&pd_rd_r=ab66c736-e734-45a9-b760-bc55a4523a49&s=sporting-goods&sp_csd=d2lkZ2V0TmFtZT1zcF9kZXRhaWxfdGhlbW F0aWM. Accessed 12 Oct. 2024.

Amazon.Com : Onyx Kayak Fishing Life Jacket : Sports & Outdoors. https://www.amazon.com/Onyx-Kayak-Fishing-

Life-Jacket/dp/B01KVRAFS8/ref=sr_1_5_mod_primary_new?crid=37V3BOOXY072Y&dib=eyJ2IjoiMSJ9.NvdaCNcBymyl8CEFQCfSaHT5YhyDfigDtl0wl_7GCn-1RcIvfVFflSkDaPkdEu9TEGIqV0URbJkLp6mlkBLzRS_Kcrudj LIxpjw9JGgPRU-QcRDaQ6uy8ozbBFwm8sjevi3t8cDR6IXH7Xs4Oi92HO3rIctETXy3YC-VQ9tJkzzdWn0POUIF2E-wCfoQTzaLUqDmkUGtk6FrZSuLGYeZsmYoDhHwvAmOhuBr-6PERaaMwcp5kFBzOknrstBXe5GsmUCMmA0FvHdUwy6BudjT8IcgGh2YNW3imMgwxAGOUo.EGNqPHk-ewEuPncYap1iY5GBeXiI5iXdBqzWNKKNEPM&dib_tag=se&keywords=Onyx-Kayak-Fishing-Life-Jacket&qid=1728093041&sbo=RZvfv%2F%2FHxDF%2BO5021pAnSA%3D%3D&sprefix=onyx-kayak-fishing-life-jacket%2Caps%2C208&sr=8-5&th=1. Accessed 12 Oct. 2024.

Amazon.Com: Pelican Sit-on-Top Kayak Scupper Plugs 4 Pack - Fits Most Kayak - EVA Material - Black : Sports & Outdoors. https://www.amazon.com/Pelican-Boats-Sit-Top-Universal/dp/B07JC2YWKK/ref=sr_1_5_pp?dib=eyJ2IjoiMSJ9.xotDsaoAulliGb8q8ku62lKx7ZOJBJ9QK-J4j9geD_DziAvf1tNDLwZmMnm7pqwSZi2AghEX1iZBsykyAV58u-dlEy3O9jSvl2v7gk-a5izoQd4sKtPe48aMkd1dquHQRm2wlOqw_Ux0l0GF3o3d24UC-TV_0InoBDv5n_kyEWviFtIIR0ZD75o1fi8WcBYtQtnZiJAUum1EKI6dHn5Foy--0h-dal8-e2Mt3RpRXQ9CKbqPnxText2jHggn2iT2fX9F-E3mtm8Dko_YHL6OzrlefdZxv0EMEeSfmonegzo.aPIOTDEBp3lrXyotITlIZpnuncsgdbc99_lSG4iEao&dib_tag=se&keywords=scupper%2Bplugs&qid=1728004698&sr=8-5&th=1. Accessed 12 Oct. 2024.

Amazon.Com: Premium Kayak Canoe Anchor Trolley System - Ultimate Rigging for Water Sports : Sports & Outdoors. https://www.amazon.com/Premium-Kayak-Anchor-Trolley-System/dp/B0CSYYKBTK/ref=sr_1_53?crid=1CDZ8DM1OO6WC&dib=eyJ2IjoiMSJ9.Io-0oM5DN-nxs4GtiQsKat_Jo5rYGXsHMAPmWcy3ioZ-OC80V8uVwUIrvE0-T6gnxVpIvq5bWtqxAtdepKzABjFqOvSl9Q7VI5oNuhKS8mXIMJWJXt2qImdywoQrawEguLnwcF9RPfGR8U87Xw60WHl4OMbmJ1xCCVDEkbNwcKnBLqVsIOvElJ853hTjOwFAtZnCZbxZ1VXKH51YxrSeXFWVRGlz8I2chIIUFdwTIXYAdF8IjXXs3AuGNUiPRuu3sjGOJq-DMWnN11JswUYVYer1nU0x-Mxj2HSjB2Am0Uc.kZ5_G88E59m5pWrNEkdlP-VwZx5_JiXwRdUFhHM_BP4&dib_tag=se&keywords=kayak+anchor+trolley+system&qid=1728093686&sprefix=kayak+anchor+trolleysystem%2Caps%2C381&sr=8-53. Accessed 12 Oct. 2024.

Amazon.Com : RAD Sportz Wall Hanger Pro Kayak and Stand Up Paddle Board Foam Padded SUP Rack : Sports & Outdoors. https://www.amazon.com/1220-Wall-Hanger-Pro-Kayak/dp/B076BVSYC5/ref=sr_1_9?crid=3VDUMOPD2LSUD&dib=eyJ2IjoiMSJ9.jXBNDVRxWgyWVouUL6jIa_ecu2fC8ehRRT7Hl0Zm3k7D0gufmFPcNxBikWkgwGspk5HlSeaaAHg2j2Lw141gOrDYPmmXbq7ylXkG2O4SQb1f_1PrDIxdJWupgxDSnPNBgac0_ouc22bwYV7ENwMlNmUSolRk9NRUHeqSWYhlASB7LqhO4b79tKSQl1dZkhQ24u4lLPMHhoMTaYunwz-yM9h1DGw8_u5CIXQjS_1c-

tTZsCYY0D_Qh1bAGqnqLgW0dHfspj282SP0ii2l4WQilJsct
TbQa8ckqEUuDhhZMGE.zXczlELhVvSNFXWB1wwF-
0BJrPvWB2Sv0ZEykA_7m1U&dib_tag=se&keywords=indo
or%2Bkayak%2Bstorage%2Brack&qid=1728094909&sprefix
=indoor%2Bkayak%2Bstorage%2Brack%2Caps%2C206&sr=
8-9&th=1. Accessed 12 Oct. 2024.

*Amazon.Com: Scotty #230-GR Power Lock Rod Holder
(Grey) : Sports & Outdoors.*
https://www.amazon.com/Scotty-230-GR-Power-Lock-
Holder/dp/B0011TTFHS/ref=sr_1_1?crid=31SUJZO8LG6
T9&dib=eyJ2IjoiMSJ9.9lw51ECbRGBCsqMztdQQveDcDmg
dugnCqZXDYxeTGX4AxSNpsFllTwgyVN8gTBsQohvFyI2iB
UbETjwUKpD3tZ-
t2oi3a5yz6VkklCZUmzjc90NGKXXnW_TBmM5qRrigKZDq
UyHStFeEyCDTkCtf6o0rhQbMUTo_JnVFxpc5J_zieEMGT4
8nkyJQMv-38eD1LcWaes59t6g5udYNl1NK5-
mLI_jXVihh2H0PZqz_2VkhyXuOMxIFBG1Tb6kL0V6zG0e
O7SmFVFMx2Ix1zE69CqYC7NnGe7VS1VkPlituwxw.1Ams
OVFTNFm0F-
D_CNFL8oAd5YQTU7TvJ0GghB4M420&dib_tag=se&keyw
ords=Scotty-230-GR-Power-Lock-
Holder&qid=1728093140&sprefix=scotty-230-gr-power-
lock-holder%2Caps%2C249&sr=8-1&th=1. Accessed 12 Oct.
2024.

*Amazon.Com : SEACHOICE Folding Grapnel Anchor 1-1/2
Lbs. 41050, Steel : Boating Anchors : Sports & Outdoors.*
https://www.amazon.com/dp/B005NI4R4E?ref=emc_s_m
_5_i_atc&th=1. Accessed 12 Oct. 2024.

*Amazon.Com: Sebnux Battery Boat Light Bow and Stern
Portable Battery Power Boat Navigation Ligt for Pontoon
and Small Boat (Black) : Sports & Outdoors.*

https://www.amazon.com/Sebnux-Battery-Portable-Navigation-Pontoon/dp/B09P1PLQ7B/ref=sr_1_1?crid=11F081O6NIW9U&dib=eyJ2IjoiMSJ9.yH-RRwvRRX9xP1xk5UavQhVlmVPx4mCNl8Ax_DCIr2U.4CvEh5uG_gMj4jQBAdEOwAF9OB8AVrJIsuMfyolGclQ&dib_tag=se&keywords=Sebnux-Battery-Portable-Navigation-Pontoon&qid=1728093388&s=sporting-goods&sprefix=sebnux-battery-portable-navigation-pontoon%2Csporting%2C184&sr=1-1&th=1. Accessed 12 Oct. 2024.

Amazon.Com : STAR BRITE Ultimate Paddlesports Cleaner & Protectant With PTEF - 22 OZ (096022) : Boating Equipment : Sports & Outdoors. https://www.amazon.com/Star-Brite-Ultimate-Paddlesports-Protectant/dp/B00EVILL2S/ref=sr_1_3?crid=BCI3YMQUGG1E&dib=eyJ2IjoiMSJ9.ZEomeuBWILQeN9hGWVXLZzWWJIm0tVg564ysn6GYOwaIhs7lCuPJmB6VvWxhSf70YBr4Uk3TYGKDd5PoDeBzkBVSEhoO1ZnGlWTDW7RQ2LBYzRePNZ3c9M90BF2-m3nHF7H3OQQa-3koQb2pEue0hu3zL0R7J58LB_f3sNGoZ8GD249eeOxUW0K2uFHQZDBX-p6nT0TMmge3gn2J6JngEJFYLu2xsF9XfTLdgeLbvdG9UU7AAwfDdeY4QMJrPI4bIvbBEpFvtllDra9n6Io7tsh_JV6j3OMq-s2rr649DG4.ODRDDky-vTCmn5Spz3F5MsosWfJy6U6LvrJGV8ZvOyk&dib_tag=se&keywords=uv+protectant+spray+for+kayaks&qid=1728094834&sprefix=uv+protectant+spray+for+kayaks%2Caps%2C231&sr=8-3. Accessed 12 Oct. 2024.

Amazon.Com : WONITAGO Stretchable Kayak Paddle Leash, Coiled Rod Leash Tool Lanyard for Kayak and SUP Paddles, Fishing Poles Rods, 1 Pack : Sports & Outdoors. https://www.amazon.com/Neolife-Stretchable-Lanyard-Paddles-Fishing/dp/B081LCTVSV/ref=sxin_16_pa_sp_search_the matic_sspa?content-id=amzn1.sym.140400a7-1208-46ad-8d2a-eb6e8eac81b5%3Aamzn1.sym.140400a7-1208-46ad-8d2a-eb6e8eac81b5&cv_ct_cx=kayak%2Bleash&dib=eyJ2IjoiMSJ9.YFjJQh-pvq5KjakvetSNWxV1we0v9dVj2uEpeaORtXLMmRRT4Ovvsd0FvZILSr3BxcXjI-Jk4B29hCVItOdwqkU0qSHyPR2cvQFl3ioXrkc.-PlzSx_lOsxjTWWZHNOH2TKsCyJ28ItqlQrs8fOpHvA&dib_tag=se&hvadid=580629915754&hvdev=c&hvlocphy=9189977&hvnetw=g&hvqmt=e&hvrand=18423309135606653179&hvtargid=kwd-2743776215&hydadcr=1138_1014978155&keywords=kayak%2Bleash&pd_rd_i=B081LCTVSV&pd_rd_r=ebc87c8d-841a-4edf-a1bf-5680541926a5&pd_rd_w=xcFdp&pd_rd_wg=MxXE1&pf_rd_p=140400a7-1208-46ad-8d2a-eb6e8eac81b5&pf_rd_r=33XRC1F9J36Y8HDVHH4N&qid=1728156334&sbo=RZvfv%2F%2FHxDF%2BO5021pAnSA%3D%3D&sr=1-4-6024b2a3-78e4-4fed-8fed-e1613be3bcce-spons&sp_csd=d2lkZ2V0TmFtZT1zcF9zZWFyY2hfdGhlbWF0aWM%3D&th=1. Accessed 12 Oct. 2024.

Amazon.Com: YakAttack ParkNPole 6' Stakeout Pole : Sports & Outdoors. https://www.amazon.com/Yakattack-Parknpole-Stakeout-Pole-

Pnp6/dp/B00HSIRRR6/ref=sr_1_2?crid=N23DEQMDB4S
6&dib=eyJ2IjoiMSJ9.DR3ZJoE9z8n6-
ejhz_WHYLdFeHzXqtW_wxWIfKFuHJpSbCQaLVtqODQ0h
natvyKqBi5XU8u-
OoepuY3hmy5awwKV0uceh5pm6tnIU5VK_g59CaiTYNg0lg
hkudDDeA7Dud2PJ7fV_sLFbQ6wH6VWc5w3w4fhtYfg4daI
KYSx-ek-
pOuWCy1cwFwuV9kjNr9KRCGlrV03GPt6s8jpu0hJnYDpv5
C9CU0VtFUxt1wvrGbywVWwgpR9enUtRAUBY7393qRk2s
ZCNjWJ6jzyn2ZXrc7fn7ci4YQGURKe61iNQrs.EuMu1eUG
MgW5F1NzokTN2tOXuvoGshqUjvwQq_HX21w&dib_tag=s
e&keywords=Yakattack-Parknpole-Stakeout-
Pole&qid=1728093588&sprefix=yakattack-parknpole-
stakeout-pole%2Caps%2C221&sr=8-2&th=1&psc=1.
Accessed 12 Oct. 2024.

"Ascend FS128T Review – Should You Buy This Fishing
Kayak?" *HappinessWithout*,
https://www.happinesswithout.com/ascend-fs128t-review/.
Accessed 19 Oct. 2024.

"Definition of Barbless Hook • FlyFish Circle." *FlyFish Circle*,
https://flyfishcircle.com/glossary/b/barbless-hook.
Accessed 12 Oct. 2024.

HandRoll – Yakima. https://yakima.com/products/handroll.
Accessed 12 Oct. 2024.

Home - Leave No Trace - Leave No Trace. https://lnt.org/.
Accessed 12 Oct. 2024.

How to Hold a Fish: 13 Steps (with Pictures) - WikiHow.
https://www.wikihow.com/Hold-a-Fish. Accessed 12 Oct.
2024.

"*How to Launch a Kayak | REI Co-Op.*" *REI*, https://www.rei.com/learn/expert-advice/kayak-launch.html. Accessed 12 Oct. 2024.

McCall, Meg. "What Is the Best Type of Kayak Paddle to Buy?" *Angle Oar*, 29 June 2023, https://www.angleoar.com/post/what-is-the-best-type-of-kayak-paddle-to-buy.

Technology, Celerant. *Pelican Argo 100x Exo Kayak.* https://www.atkenco.com/pelican/pelican-argo-100x-exo-kayak-68022. Accessed 20 Oct. 2024.

Thule Hullavator Pro | Thule | United States. https://www.thule.com/en-us/water-racks/kayak-and-canoe-racks/thule-hullavator-pro-_-1685448. Accessed 12 Oct. 2024.

"Wilderness Systems Tarpon 105 Sit-On-Top Fishing Kayak - 10'6"." *REI Co-Op*, https://www.rei.com/product/170834/wilderness-systems-tarpon-105-sit-on-top-fishing-kayak-106. Accessed 19 Oct. 2024.

www.ingramcontent.com/pod-product-compliance
Lightning Source LLC
Chambersburg PA
CBHW060252030426
42335CB00014B/1657